THE PATRIARCHS
AND MOSES

THE BIBLE
AND
ITS STORY

1
THE CREATION

2
THE PATRIARCHS
AND MOSES

3
IN THE PROMISED LAND

4
KINGS AND PROPHETS

5
EXILE AND RETURN

6
JESUS THE CHRIST

7
THE LORD'S FOLLOWERS

Planned and produced by
Jaca Book-Centurion
from the ideas of
Charles Ehlinger, Hervé Lauriot Prévost,
Pierre Talec, and the editorial committee
of Jaca Book

A chapter outline for this volume
is printed on the last two pages
of the volume.

THE PATRIARCHS AND MOSES

THE BIBLE AND ITS STORY

Text by Pierre Talec
Translation by Kenneth D. Whitehead
Illustration by Antonio Molino

 Winston Press   430 Oak Grove   Minneapolis, Minnesota 55403

Published in Italy under the title
I Patriarchi E Mosé
Copyright © 1981 Jaca Book-Centurion

**Licensed publisher and distributor
of the English-language edition:**
Winston Press, Inc.
430 Oak Grove
Minneapolis, Minnesota 55403
United States of America

Agents:
Canada—
LeDroit/Novalis-Select
135 Nelson Street
Ottawa, Ontario
Canada K1N 7R4

Australia, New Zealand, New Guinea, Fiji Islands—
Dove Communications, Pty. Ltd.
Suite 1   60-64 Railway Road
Blackburn, Victoria 3130
Australia

Acknowledgements:
All Scripture quotations, unless otherwise
indicated, are taken from the *Revised
Standard Version Common Bible*, copyright ©
1973 by the Division of Christian Education
of the National Council of the Churches of
Christ in the U.S.A. Used by permission.

All Scripture quotations indicated by *TEV*
(Today's English Version) are from the
Good News Bible - Old Testament: Copyright ©
American Bible Society 1976; New Testament:
Copyright © American Bible Society, 1966,
1971, 1976.

Winston Scriptural Consultant:
Catherine Litecky, CSJ
Department of Theology
College of St. Catherine

Winston Staff:
Lois Welshons, Hermann Weinlick - editorial
Reg Sandland, Kathe Wilcoxon - design

Jaca Book-Centurion Editorial Committee:
Maretta Campi, Charles Ehlinger,
Enrico Galbiati, Elio Guerriero, Pierre Talec

Color selection: Carlo Scotti, Milan
Printing: Gorenjski tisk, Kranj, Yugoslavia

Library of Congress Catalog Card Number: 82-050637
ISBN: 0-86683-192-4

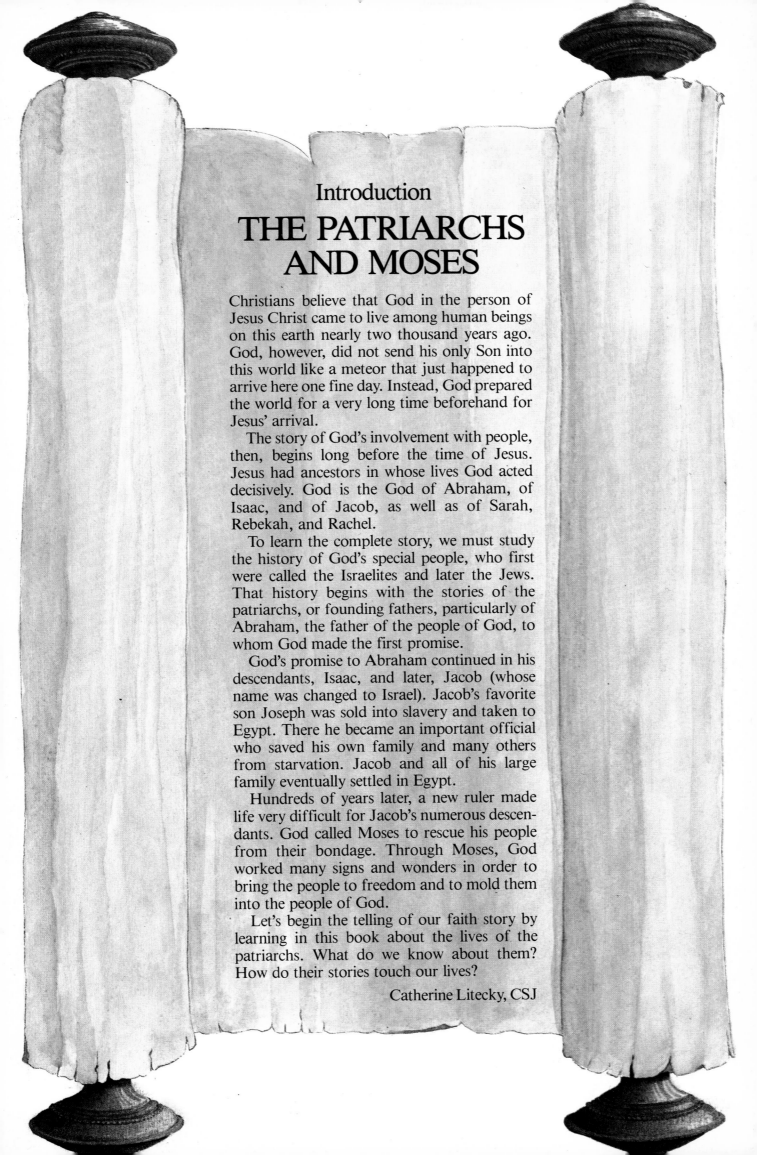

Introduction

THE PATRIARCHS AND MOSES

Christians believe that God in the person of Jesus Christ came to live among human beings on this earth nearly two thousand years ago. God, however, did not send his only Son into this world like a meteor that just happened to arrive here one fine day. Instead, God prepared the world for a very long time beforehand for Jesus' arrival.

The story of God's involvement with people, then, begins long before the time of Jesus. Jesus had ancestors in whose lives God acted decisively. God is the God of Abraham, of Isaac, and of Jacob, as well as of Sarah, Rebekah, and Rachel.

To learn the complete story, we must study the history of God's special people, who first were called the Israelites and later the Jews. That history begins with the stories of the patriarchs, or founding fathers, particularly of Abraham, the father of the people of God, to whom God made the first promise.

God's promise to Abraham continued in his descendants, Isaac, and later, Jacob (whose name was changed to Israel). Jacob's favorite son Joseph was sold into slavery and taken to Egypt. There he became an important official who saved his own family and many others from starvation. Jacob and all of his large family eventually settled in Egypt.

Hundreds of years later, a new ruler made life very difficult for Jacob's numerous descendants. God called Moses to rescue his people from their bondage. Through Moses, God worked many signs and wonders in order to bring the people to freedom and to mold them into the people of God.

Let's begin the telling of our faith story by learning in this book about the lives of the patriarchs. What do we know about them? How do their stories touch our lives?

Catherine Litecky, CSJ

1 Abraham, our ancestor in faith,
was the first patriarch.
He and his family were
desert nomads, tending
flocks of sheep and goats.
Stories about Abraham
and other patriarchs were told
by one generation to the next.
Many years later, scribes
wrote the stories down,
in order to preserve them
and to remind the people
about God's faithfulness.

Recently an ancient boundary-post was discovered in the desert, uncovered by the winds. On it was written a name that makes us think of a particular person. The name was Abram. So far, this name on the post is the only existing thing we have, besides the Bible, that might mention the biblical Abraham.

Does the name on this ancient desert boundary-post really refer to the patriarch of the Bible? Probably not. The name Abram may have been as familiar then as Bill or Lisa is in our day.

It's true that we have all the stories the Bible tells us about Abraham. In fact, the Bible tells quite a few stories about his life.

But telling stories is not the same thing as writing history. In order to write history we need to have exhibits, just as at a trial. We need written documents or evidence that we can prove is true, for example, an inscription on a monument. But we don't have any evidence such as this dating from the time of Abraham.

How much is simply legend in the stories the Bible tells about Abraham? Because we modern people are so used to scientific investigation, the serious Christian today isn't satisfied merely

with marvelous tales. He or she asks questions and wants to get to the bottom of things. So, if we consider believable history to be only those things which can be proven by existing evidence or written documents, then we must consider the life of Abraham and the patriarchs as belonging to prehistory, rather than to history.

How did the stories found in the Bible come down to us? How did they get to be included in the texts of the Book of Genesis, the first book in the Bible? Far back in history, desert nomads often told each other stories in the evening by the light of their little terra-cotta lamps, while the moon cast its reflection on the sides of their goatskin tents. Stories such as those about Abraham were very old stories. They were told and retold orally over many generations. This process of telling and retelling is what we call a living tradition. What a shame it would have been if such marvelous stories had simply been lost or forgotten. That is why a very long time after the stories were first told—around the tenth century B.C., in fact, under Solomon—these same stories finally were written down by scribes (people who could write). This was when biblical writing, that is, "Scripture," developed. The tradition of writing things down continued.

As time went by, scribes revised and reworked the traditional stories, because new generations of people interpreted the stories in the light of their own experiences. During the exile of the Jews in Babylon, for example, the people of Israel, who had been forced to leave their homeland, became downcast and despairing. "We were unfaithful to our covenant with the Lord God Yahweh," they told themselves. "That is why God has abandoned us here." "Not so," the Jewish priests replied. "It isn't possible that God has abandoned us, because God is faithful to his word. Surely you remember the promises God made to Abraham!" So in the sixth century B.C., in order to provide support and comfort for the Jewish exiles, the traditions about the lives of Abraham and the patriarchs were written down. In this way, the people were reminded of God's faithfulness.

Just as Abraham had faith and confidence in the promises of God, so we Christians have confidence in the Word of God in the Bible. Faith does not depend on our being able to prove historically people and events.

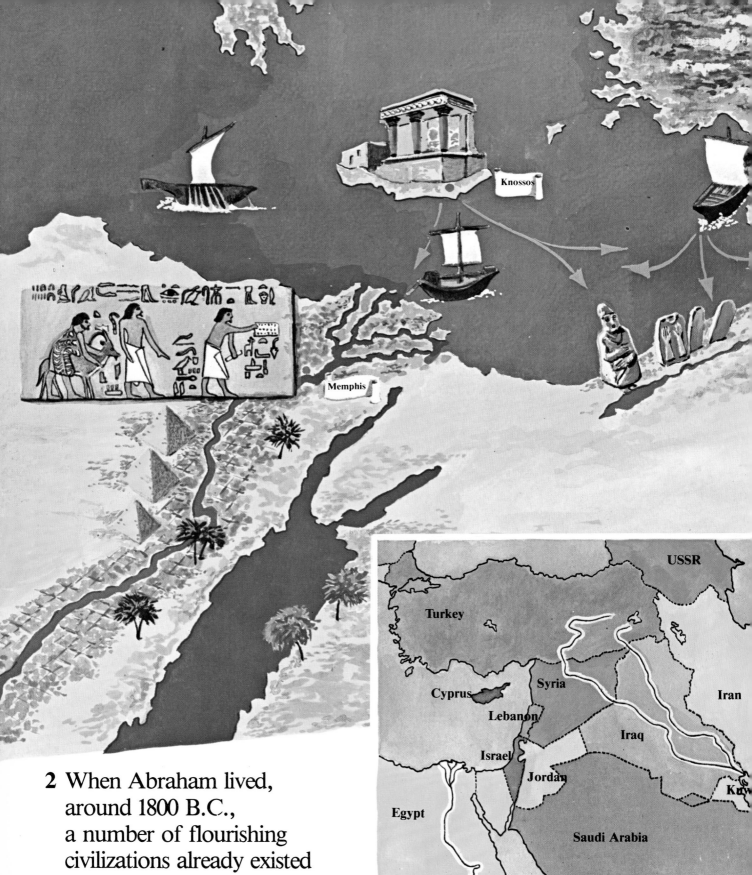

2 When Abraham lived,
around 1800 B.C.,
a number of flourishing
civilizations already existed
in the Middle East.

Ur, Haran, Canaan, and Egypt — all are places on Abraham's long journey. If we glance at a map of the Middle East and join together all these places, we see that they form a curve that resembles the blade of a sickle or a crescent-shaped moon. This curve, commonly called the Fertile Crescent, is the cradle of civilization in the Near East.

At one end of the crescent is an immense plain through which the Tigris and Euphrates rivers flow. This is called Mesopotamia, or "the land between the two rivers." In this region the first cities were built, among them the city of Ur.

At the other end of the Fertile Crescent lie the delta and the valley of the Nile: a long, narrow band of green, fertile land wedged in between two arid desert plateaus. This valley formed ancient Egypt — land of pyramids and great stone temples.

It was in Mesopotamia, the land of the ancient Sumerians with its capital city of Ur, that writing was invented around 3000 B.C.

This writing is called "cuneiform" (wedge-shaped) writing; today it is found on many surviving clay tablets.

In Egypt, a little later, a type of writing called "hieroglyphics" (picture writing) was invented. This writing is found carved into many Egyptian monuments.

Between Egypt and Mesopotamia, extending along the Mediterranean coast, lay the land of Canaan. It consisted of Palestine and Phoenicia. In Phoenicia, around 1500 B.C., the first real alphabet was invented. It was a clear and simple system of writing that the Phoencians taught the Greeks, and the Greeks passed on to the entire Western world. The invention of writing made it possible to write history. And from this written history we get some idea about Abraham's world.

In Abraham's time, besides Ur these cities were prominent: Babylon, north of Ur; Mari, on the middle Euphrates; and, a little further east, on the Tigris, Asshur, the city that gave its name to Assyria.

The Hittites were already living in Asia Minor but had not yet reached the peak of their power. The cities on the Phoenician coast were already prospering, particularly Byblos, which furnished Egypt with wood cut from the cedars of Lebanon. In Canaan, the second part of Abraham's journeying, there existed some small fortified cities, including Shechem, Hebron, and Jerusalem. These cities ruled the surrounding countryside, but there still remained vast open spaces where nomads roamed, and where Abraham pitched his tents. Nomads called "Amurru" by the inhabitants of Ur and Babylon also wandered in these areas. This word meant "westerners," and they were called by this name because they came from the steppes west of the Euphrates. We call them Amorites.

Just before Abraham's time, some warring bands of Amorites had conquered the cities of Mesopotamia and established dynasties, or ruling families, in these cities. The most famous dynasty, in Babylon, included the well-known leader, Hammurabi, who ordered carved on stones one of humanity's most ancient codes of law. Other bands of Amorite nomads were peaceful shepherds. Abraham's family was among them.

3 Abram lived on the steppes
outside of Ur,
a large city in Mesopotamia.
He traded his flocks' products
for wheat, barley, and oil.
Just as all nomads did,
Abram's family joined with
other families to form a tribe.

When we read in the Bible that Abram (later called Abraham) was a native of Ur, we shouldn't think of him actually living in the busy city. In fact, his family lived outside of Ur. His work required him to move around with his flocks of sheep and goats.

But the city was the marketplace for him to sell the products of his animals and to purchase the things that he needed: wheat, barley, oil, ceramic jars and dishes, and other necessities.

Nomads, then as now, had their own kind of independent organization based on the extended family. The father of this family, called the "patriarch," or head of the family, exercised complete authority over the families of his sons and nephews. He also was in charge of all the slaves, who were part of the extended family and were needed to help in grazing the animals. These flocks of sheep and goats were the nomad family's wealth, although camels and donkeys were also kept.

Usually several patriarchal families, united by blood or pledged to one another for safety, formed larger, tribal groupings. Marriages took place within the tribe.

Imagine Abram as a boy living this nomadic existence, accompanying the shepherds out on the steppes, visiting the marketplaces of Ur with his father, or sitting near the tents on summer evenings, listening to the stories told by the elders. This peaceful way of life involved constant contact with nature, either beneath the burning sun shining on the endless plains or exposed to the rare rainstorms. These storms, occurring at the end of the brief winters, produced, as if by magic, a short-lived covering of countless yellow, violet, and scarlet desert flowers.

Being so close to nature probably made it easier for Abram to think about his God, and to imagine God as living beyond the spangled heavens of starry desert nights. Out on the steppes one could sense that God had to be immense and without the sort of faces carved for the gods that people adored in the temples of Ur.

Abram was the first of the real "Friends of God": the first of the people God selected as part of the divine plan for the salvation of human beings. Perhaps Abram came to know God, in some mysterious fashion, while he was still quite young. It could have been a special voice, different from the usual whistling of the wind, echoing inside of him as much as in his ears, that made him aware of the presence of the invisible God. Or maybe something prompted Abram, while he was meditating, to ask "Who is God?" When the time was right, the God so long desired would make himself known to Abram.

4 Ur, built along the Euphrates,
was the center
of a prosperous civilization.
It contained a large tower,
or ziggurat, built
in honor of the moon god.
Abram's family left Ur
to move north, to Haran.

Ur had already existed about two thousand years when Abram was born. Already three different dynasties had ruled over it and the surrounding towns. The splendor of the last dynasty was still fresh in people's minds.

Even from a distance, only a glance was required in order to see, on the horizon, Ur's ziggurat, an enormous tower with steps. (It's still standing today, four thousand years after Abraham.) It took only a glance to be reminded of the power of the king Ur-Nammu, who had commanded this step tower built in honor of the moon god, who was the guardian god of the city.

The city of Ur was still a holy city in Abram's time, even though the greatest power had passed to other cities or dynasties, such as those of Isin or Laksa. Babylon in Abram's time was on its way to achieving the great power it would possess a century later through Hammurabi's conquests.

The city of Ur itself was still a marvel. It contained great temples, a royal palace, and many administrative buildings. Private houses made of solid stone were commonly built two stories high. The streets were straight and well maintained. The temples were centers of commerce; they were filled with agricultural products from fields watered by the vast network of irrigation canals that surrounded the city. The waters of the Euphrates River brought to the edge of the city boats filled with merchandise from the Persian Gulf. The writing on thousands of the ancient clay tablets which we possess today recorded Ur's commercial transactions. Contracts were written down, signed, and sealed; records of debts were carefully kept.

On other clay tablets are written myths, hymns, and prayers to the gods. The Sumerian religion, out of which the religions of Babylonia and Assyria grew, took for granted the existence of many gods, who were represented in human form. The principal gods were these three: An, the god of the sky; Enlil, the god of the air; and Enki, the god of water and of wisdom. Other gods and goddesses were the heavenly bodies: the moon god (Nanna, Sin); the sun god (Utu, Shamash), who was the moon's son; and the planet Venus, the "morning star" (Ianna). Ianna was a fertility goddess whom the Babylonians later called Ishtar and the Canaanites called Astarte.

In addition to these gods were the guardian gods of each city or town. Each family also honored its own household, or personal, gods. This particular practice was widespread among the Amorites; often their names coupled the name of a god with a family name.

At some point, Abram's family, led by Abram's father Terah and accompanied by all of their flocks and slaves, left Ur and journeyed

all the way to the city of Haran. This six-hundred-mile journey was through the steppes along the banks of the Euphrates. It probably took several years, with the family setting up many camps along the way and stopping often for the flocks to graze.

5 Abram and his wife Sarai,
along with his father's family,
lived outside of Haran.
One day, the Lord
commanded Abram, saying
"Leave your native land
and your people
and go to a far country."
Without argument or doubt,
Abram obeyed.
His obedience is the beginning
of our long faith story.

It was a long time ago, perhaps as long ago as around the year 1800 B.C. and at least as long ago as 1400 B.C., that a certain man, along with his family, moved north from Ur. The Bible tells the story. Moving up the Euphrates River, this man established his camp around Haran, the Syrian oasis town located in the land the Bible calls "Aram." Haran, on the regular caravan route, was a busy trade center. Its inhabitants were Amorites, so they belonged to the same race as the family of Abram.

The man who came to Haran was called Abram; later he would be called Abraham. He was an important chief, or sheikh, respected among the nomad tribes. The Book of Genesis says that his father's name was Terah and that his two brothers were named Nahor and Haran. Haran had a son, Lot, who was a very beloved nephew of Abram. Abram's wife was called Sarai.

With his large family and his many flocks, Abram lived for a while around Haran. He ranged in an area in northern Mesopotamia, land which today makes up the extreme south of Turkey, near the Syrian border. Although he was originally from Ur, Abram has been traditionally regarded as coming from around Haran. Certainly he did live there for a while—and his sheep and goats had plenty of opportunity to get fattened up.

Abram worshiped the gods that were honored in the countries where he lived. He was a man of silence, a man of the desert. He was accustomed to the starry skies, and he knew how to listen in the night. And one day a voice made itself heard, a voice that seemed to come from somewhere beyond. It was the voice of Yahweh (one of the names given to the Lord God in the Bible). This is what the voice of Yahweh told Abram, according to the Book of Genesis:

"Leave your native land, your relatives,
and your father's home,
and go to a country
that I am going to show you.
I will give you many descendants,
and they will become a great nation.
I will bless you
and make your name famous,
so that you will be a blessing.
I will bless those
who bless you,
but I will curse those
who curse you.
And through you I will bless
all the nations." (Genesis 12:1-3 TEV)

At the age of seventy-five, without having to be urged further, Abram departed for the unknown: the land of Canaan. The absolute trust and confidence in Yahweh that Abram showed, his obedience to God's voice without raising his own voice, is the main reason that he has earned the admiration of Jews, Christians, and Muslims alike. His faith was all the more remarkable in that he did not "know" God as we now know God through his revealing himself in Jesus.

John reports in his Gospel how the Pharisees, who were experts in the law of Moses, were nevertheless proudest of being sons of Abraham; some of them scolded Jesus when they thought he was pretending to be greater than Abraham. Paul's Letter to the Hebrews in the New Testament presents Abraham as the best example of faith. And Paul explains in his Letter to the Romans how much God recognized and valued the faith of Abraham. Thus, centuries and centuries later, generations and generations after Abraham, the Christian tradition still holds up as a model for us the faith and trust shown by "Abraham, our father in faith."

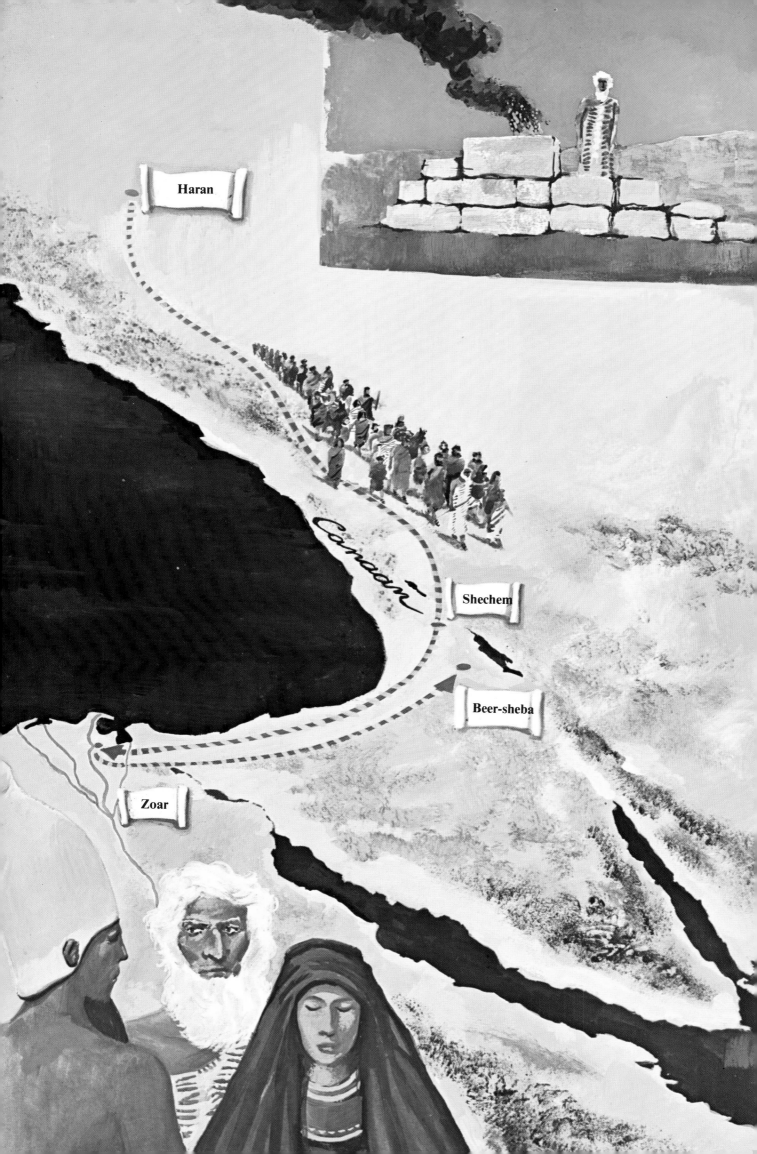

Haran

Canaan

Shechem

Beer-sheba

Zoar

6 Abram arrived in Canaan
and was able to roam it freely.
He worshiped his own God
in Canaan's holy places.
At Shechem, God promised
to give Abram the very land
in which Abram was journeying.
Abram traveled to Egypt
and remained for a while.
When back in Canaan, Abram
and his nephew Lot separated.

Around 1800 B.C.—the time, most scholars agree, that Abram's journey of faith to Canaan took place—Egypt, which had formerly ruled Canaan, was no longer strong. It was ruled by the Hyksos, nomad princes from Asia Minor. The Assyrian Empire, which later was very powerful, had not yet begun its growth. The world's great empires were not at war at that particular moment.

So this was a good time for Abram to pitch his tents in Canaan; that narrow strip of land along the Mediterranean coast was like unplowed ground, waiting to be planted. It was divided up into separate little territories, each governed by minor lords and rulers who lived in small fortified cities. Nomads grazing their flocks could pass through the country freely. Abram was able to move across Canaan without any interference.

Always a religious person, Abram on his journey visited many of the sacred places that were set aside and dedicated to local gods. But it was his God whom he worshiped in these places. Thus, at Shechem, at the Oak of Moreh, he built an altar to his God. This became a very important spot, because it was there—as the Book of Genesis relates—that Abram received God's revelation concerning the land "promised" to him. "To your descendants I will give this very land," Yahweh declared.

Abram also made stops at Bethel and Ai on his journey. These short stopovers were ways of leaving his mark, of claiming the promised land as the Lord's, although the land itself still needed to be actually conquered.

Abram then proceeded south to the famous Negev desert, an empty place where there was little food. From the Negev, Abram continued down into Egypt. And there a strange thing happened to him.

Sarai, the wife of Abram (and his half sister), was an unusually beautiful woman. Tales of her beauty came even to the ears of Pharaoh (the ruler of Egypt), who could not resist her charms. Abram had feared that Pharaoh would not be able to resist her beauty. Therefore he had said to Sarai, "Tell the Egyptians that you are my sister. Thus Pharaoh will not think he is taking my wife, and he will leave me alone." Thus it happened.

But Pharaoh ended up regretting his actions after all. He became afflicted with a skin disease of some sort for having taken Abram's wife, even though he didn't realize who she was. He later discovered the trick and scolded Abram for having deceived him. As a result of all this, Abram had to leave Egypt and head back towards the Negev and back to Bethel and Ai. He took Sarai back with him.

Once back in Canaan, the herdsmen of Abram and Lot began to bicker with one another over pasture lands. Lands that they'd used before were no longer large enough for the herds of both men.

"We should not be quarreling," Abram told Lot. "There is plenty of land. Let us each take different parts."

Lot agreed to this reasonable proposal and moved his herds southeast, towards the city of Sodom. Abram moved his herds to the south and established himself around the town of Hebron. Here, once more, God renewed his promise to Abram that he would be the father of a great people. Abram pitched his tents in the shade of the oaks of Mamre, where his flocks could find pastures.

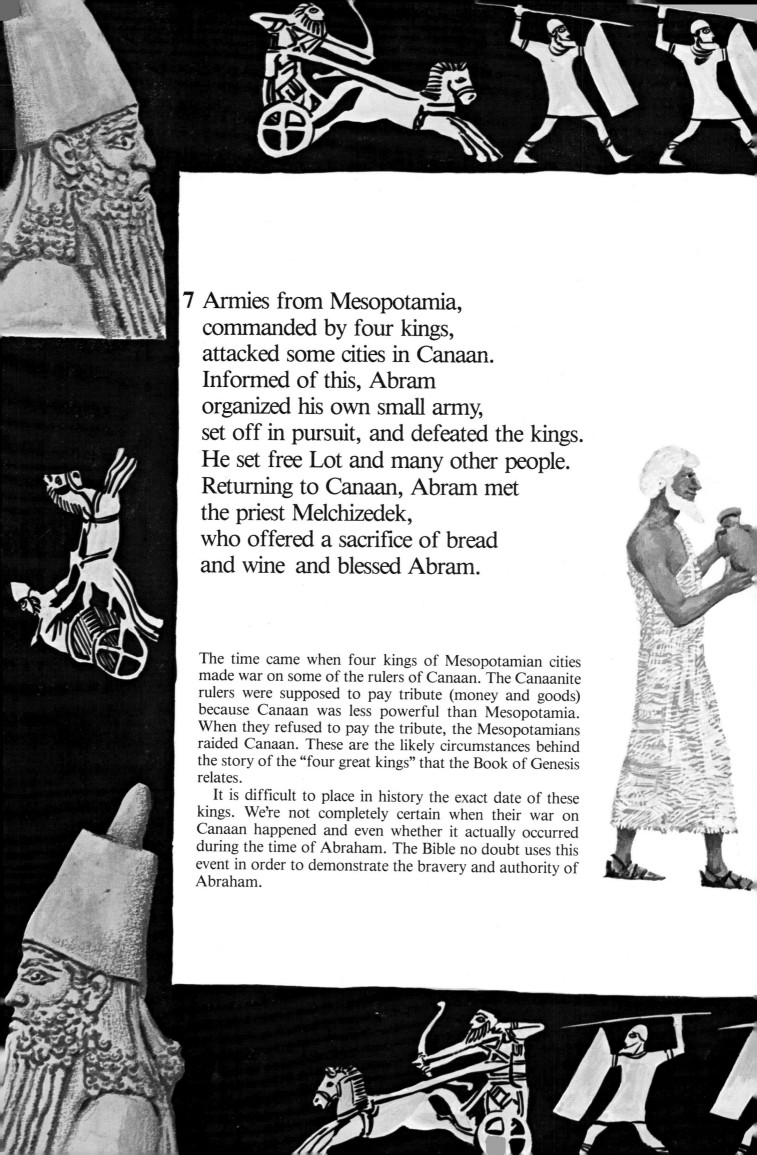

7 Armies from Mesopotamia,
commanded by four kings,
attacked some cities in Canaan.
Informed of this, Abram
organized his own small army,
set off in pursuit, and defeated the kings.
He set free Lot and many other people.
Returning to Canaan, Abram met
the priest Melchizedek,
who offered a sacrifice of bread
and wine and blessed Abram.

The time came when four kings of Mesopotamian cities made war on some of the rulers of Canaan. The Canaanite rulers were supposed to pay tribute (money and goods) because Canaan was less powerful than Mesopotamia. When they refused to pay the tribute, the Mesopotamians raided Canaan. These are the likely circumstances behind the story of the "four great kings" that the Book of Genesis relates.

It is difficult to place in history the exact date of these kings. We're not completely certain when their war on Canaan happened and even whether it actually occurred during the time of Abraham. The Bible no doubt uses this event in order to demonstrate the bravery and authority of Abraham.

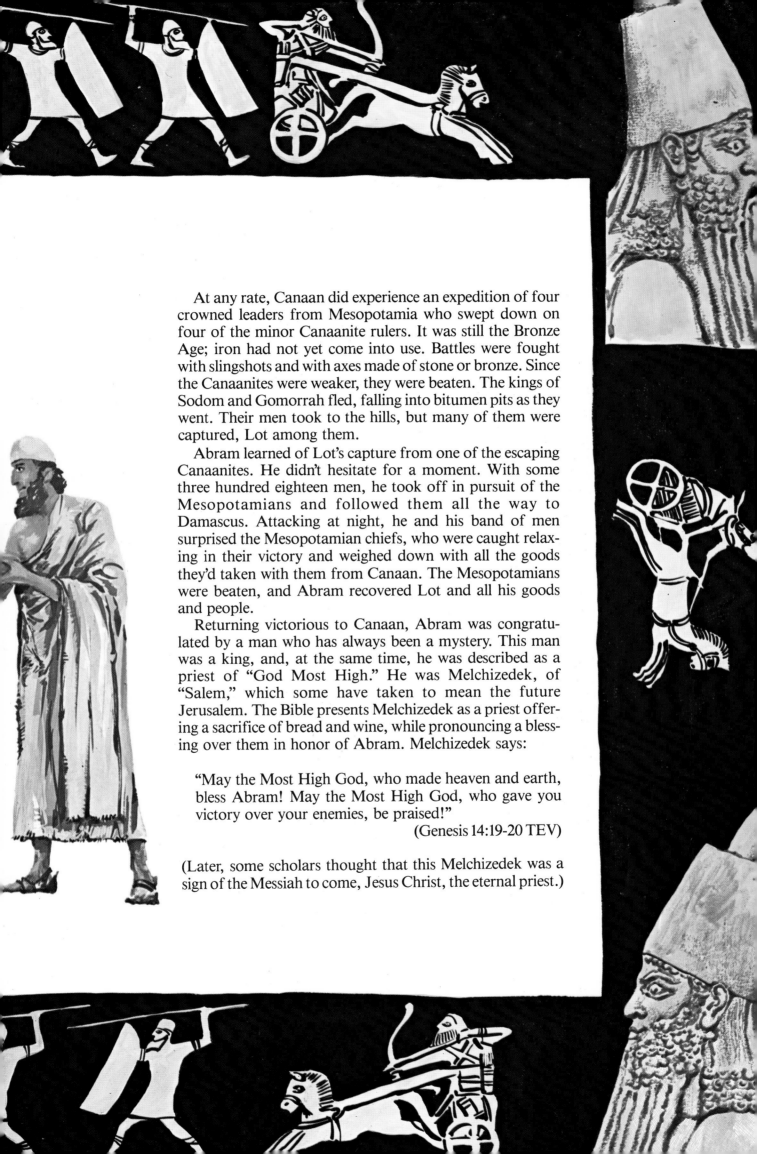

At any rate, Canaan did experience an expedition of four crowned leaders from Mesopotamia who swept down on four of the minor Canaanite rulers. It was still the Bronze Age; iron had not yet come into use. Battles were fought with slingshots and with axes made of stone or bronze. Since the Canaanites were weaker, they were beaten. The kings of Sodom and Gomorrah fled, falling into bitumen pits as they went. Their men took to the hills, but many of them were captured, Lot among them.

Abram learned of Lot's capture from one of the escaping Canaanites. He didn't hesitate for a moment. With some three hundred eighteen men, he took off in pursuit of the Mesopotamians and followed them all the way to Damascus. Attacking at night, he and his band of men surprised the Mesopotamian chiefs, who were caught relaxing in their victory and weighed down with all the goods they'd taken with them from Canaan. The Mesopotamians were beaten, and Abram recovered Lot and all his goods and people.

Returning victorious to Canaan, Abram was congratulated by a man who has always been a mystery. This man was a king, and, at the same time, he was described as a priest of "God Most High." He was Melchizedek, of "Salem," which some have taken to mean the future Jerusalem. The Bible presents Melchizedek as a priest offering a sacrifice of bread and wine, while pronouncing a blessing over them in honor of Abram. Melchizedek says:

> "May the Most High God, who made heaven and earth, bless Abram! May the Most High God, who gave you victory over your enemies, be praised!"
> (Genesis 14:19-20 TEV)

(Later, some scholars thought that this Melchizedek was a sign of the Messiah to come, Jesus Christ, the eternal priest.)

8 God reveals himself
to people through
marvelous events in nature,
by messengers called angels,
through signs called miracles.
Stories of these occurrences
in ancient times
were told and retold,
creating various traditions,
or collections of stories.
The traditions were gathered
to form the Bible.

Yahweh, the invisible God, had to become recognizable so that people could understand when God spoke.

The biblical writers, influenced by other religions around them, were very observant of nature. They were clever and made good use of the things in nature. Things like fire. They saw that the image of fire could help people understand what God is like: Fire gives off light and heat, and it recalls the warmth of home and cooking fires. As we shall later see, Moses understood that God was revealing himself to him in the fire of a burning bush and through the flaming smoke on Mount Sinai.

There is a special word for God's dramatic manifestations through marvelous occurrences in nature. This special word is "theophany." Theophanies are occasions when God reveals himself to human beings.

How can we understand this God? God becomes recognizable, although no one can really see God. God speaks, although God has no mouth. Who can tell us what God's voice sounds like? The authors of the Bible established certain conventions (agreed upon ways of doing things) to help make God's voice heard. For instance, they report the activities of beings which the Bible calls "messengers of Yahweh"—which we translate with the word "angels." An angel is one who speaks for God, who is identified with God. Thus, when we read in the Bible "the angel of Yahweh says," we are supposed to understand that it is God speaking.

Other similar special conventions are used in the Bible: God is represented as appearing to people in sleep, in a dream, or in a vision. There are also expressions, such as "the oracle of Yahweh," that indicate that God has spoken, without explaining exactly how.

Often the gospels report marvelous things such as the calming of a storm or the raising of Lazarus from the dead. These unusual happenings are called miracles. They are found in the Bible long before Jesus' time. They are reported as occurring throughout the entire history of the people of God. Miracles are signs; they are another way in which God becomes recognizable and speaks to humankind.

But what is meant by a miracle? It is an extraordinary happening that goes beyond what could occur naturally. Science, in its present state of development, cannot explain miracles. But whether a miracle really occurred or was only believed to have occurred is not the most important thing. The most important thing about the miracles in the Bible is that they are events of faith. What really counts is that we should be open enough to God to allow ourselves to be challenged by what goes beyond our understanding.

The people who experienced theophanies and miracles were very impressed by them, of course, and they told and retold stories about

them to their families. Thus were born the first stories, the earliest traditions, which in the time of the patriarchs were purely oral, that is to say, told to others. With the passing of years, the traditions, or versions, became so numerous that it was necessary to write them down so that they wouldn't be lost. After writing became known in Palestine, the stories multiplied. Eventually the traditions were brought together and together formed the Bible. Today we distinguish four main traditions, or sources, in the Hebrew Scriptures.

The *Yahwist* source, the most ancient, was written down in the tenth century before Christ.

It is called Yahwist because in these writings God is called Yahweh.

The *Elohist* source, dating from the ninth century, gets its name because God is called Elohim, meaning "Lord."

The *Deuteronomist* source was written down at the end of the seventh century before Christ. This name comes from a Greek word meaning "second law."

The *priestly* source was written down by priests in the sixth century, probably during the Babylonian exile, and is mostly about worship.

9 God promised Abram
countless descendants
and a land to possess.
Although Abram was old
and had no son,
he believed God's promise.
God made a covenant,
or agreement, with Abram.
They sealed the covenant
by the sacrifice of animals.
The Lord God passed by
as the fire burned.

The Bible contains two versions of God's covenant with Abraham. This chapter presents the Yahwist version.

"Look toward heaven and number the stars, if you are able to number them. So shall your descendants be." Who is speaking like this?

"I am the Lord who brought you from Ur of the Chaldeans, to give you this land to possess." These words must have reached Abram in a sort of dream. Hearing a voice such as this without knowing for sure where it came from must have been rather frightening, even though Yahweh was careful first to say to Abram, "Fear not, Abram! I am your shield; your reward shall be very great."

"Your own son shall be your heir." Abram did not doubt the Lord's words. However, God's promise did present a problem for him. How could it all happen? He had no son by Sarai, and he was already an old man.

Impossible as it seemed to be, Abram, relying solely on the promise of God, believed that it would happen. His faith counted for a great deal in the sight of God. God valued highly Abram's trust and confidence, and honored Abram for it.

However, even the greatest of faith does not exclude common sense. Abram could not help asking sensible questions; he could not help going over in his mind the incredible promise: "I will give you this land to possess." He asked, "How am I to know that I shall possess it?" God, as a sign of the covenant with Abram, demanded that Abram offer the kind of sacrifice that it was customary to offer in Canaan at that time.

The Bible, in a story which originated with what we call a Yahwist source, explains precisely and in detail how Abram sacrificed a three-year-old heifer (a young cow) and a she-goat of the same age, cutting them in half and placing each half next to the other. To these animal sacrifices he added a young pigeon and a turtledove. Just as the sun was going down, at the fragile moment when dusk dissolves into the last red streaks of the darkening sky, the covenant was sealed with an old religious rite accompanied by specific words.

A rite is a religious act that is very carefully carried out in exactly the same way each time, according to set rules, in order to indicate that something completely beyond our understanding is taking place.

In the fire of Abram's sacrifice, it was not merely "something" that was taking place; the Lord God Yahweh was passing by, represented in the fire. In this kind of sacrifice, some fuel, such as a piece of straw, would catch fire and burn across from one sacrificial animal to the other. As the fire burned, as Yahweh passed, Abram knew that the covenant with God had been sealed. The accompanying words from the voice of God were: "To your descendants I give this land from the river of Egypt to the great river, the Euphrates."

This covenant with God did not resemble any pact, treaty, or agreement signed between humans; it was a unique kind of agreement of which God was the sole initiator. God alone decided to make the offer. The Bible tells us that it was in this exact way that God actively began to be involved in human history, in the destiny of the people to be built on Abraham. God planted the seed.

10 Abram grew older
and still was childless.
At Sarai's suggestion,
Abram had a son
with Hagar, Sarai's maid.
A son, Ishmael, was born
of that union.
Ishmael was protected by God,
but was not considered
the son of "the promise."

Sarai, the wife of Abram, was unable to have a child. It was a great sadness for her, and even a torment. Would Abram because of her lose the wonderful future promised by Yahweh? Sarai could not bear that possibility. After waiting patiently for ten years for the child that did not come, she had an idea that she proposed to Abram: "Go in to my maid; it may be that I shall obtain children by her." Abram agreed with this proposal, especially since the laws of his native country permitted this. (In Mesopotamia, a sterile wife had a right to "give" a maidservant to her husband in order to have children.) Thus it was that Sarai's beautiful Egyptian servant girl, Hagar, found herself pregnant by Abram. Hagar became so proud of her condition that she began to look down on Sarai. Angry at being scorned by her own servant, Sarai complained to Abram, but he simply told her to work things out as she pleased.

Thus it was that Sarai began to mistreat Hagar — so much so that the poor girl fled into the desert. The Bible reports that the angel of the Lord found Hagar near a spring on the way to Shur. The angel urged her to return to her mistress and to be submissive to her; then the angel consoled her with words which echoed the promise that the Lord had already made to Abram. But this time the promise was not made to a man, to the patriarch, but rather to a woman, and to a foreign woman at that, to an Egyptian, Hagar. This is what the angel said to her:

> "I will so greatly multiply your descendants that they cannot be numbered for multitude.... Behold, you are with child, and shall bear a son; you shall call his name Ishmael; because the Lord has given heed to your affliction. He shall be a wild ass of a man, his hand against every man and every man's hand against him...." (Genesis 16:10-12)

This prophecy of the angel is a strange one, foretelling how Hagar's son was destined to be a rebel caught up in strife and dissension. It was in these circumstances that the first son of Abram was born of Hagar in the land of Canaan, the land that would eventually become Palestine. But this first son of Abram was not his heir; he was not the ancestor of the people of Israel; rather he was the ancestor of another Semitic people related to the Jews, the Arabs. The Lord God promised to make a great nation out of the Arabs, too.

11 God once more promised that Abram would have an heir and would be the father of many, including kings. God changed Abram's name to Abraham and Sarai's name to Sarah, as a sign that they belonged to God. God asked that all of Abraham's male descendants be circumcised, as a sign of the covenant.

The Bible presents two versions of God's covenant with Abraham. This chapter is based on the priestly tradition.

When he was almost one hundred years old, Abram dreamed of God, and God appeared to him with marvelous generosity: "I am God Almighty. Walk before me and be blameless. And I will make my covenant between me and you, and will multiply you exceedingly...and kings shall come forth from you." Abram was almost overcome with this startling revelation. But that was not all. God also said to Abram: "No longer shall your name be Abram, but your name shall be Abraham. As for Sarai, your wife, you shall not call her name Sarai, but Sarah shall be her name."

Names were very important to Abram's people. To be able to give a name to someone meant to have an advantage or to have authority over him or her. That is one of the reasons the ancient Jews did not actually pronounce the name of God; they knew that nobody possesses God. In changing the names of Abram to Abraham and Sarai to Sarah, God was showing that he owned them: "I will be your God!" As the sign that Abraham's descendants would belong specially to Yahweh, God commanded that every Jewish male was to be circumcised, eight days after his birth.

Circumcision is a minor operation performed on boys in which the foreskin that covers the end of the penis is cut off. This operation on Jewish males was meant to be a sign, marked in their very flesh, testifying that they belonged to Yahweh. It was a sign of their being different from all other peoples anywhere.

Recall that the first account of the covenant in the Bible (according to the Yahwist tradition) mentions the sacrifice performed by Abram as the special "sign" of the covenant. This second account of the covenant (according to the priestly tradition) emphasizes circumcision as that "sign."

This difference in emphasis is easily explained. This second, priestly version was written by Judean priests during the Babylonian exile of the Jewish people after 586 B.C. During this exile the Jews lived among the pagan inhabitants of Babylon; they risked losing their identity, their awareness that they belonged to Yahweh in a special way. So that the Jews would always remember who they were, their priests insisted upon circumcision as a sign of their difference. Besides being a religious sign, circumcision was also important to the Jews as a sign of their uniqueness as a group of people.

The priestly account of the covenant agrees with the Yahwist account in one important way. Both accounts say that God's promise of a son to Abraham was the actual beginning of God's covenant with Abraham and with his descendants forever.

"Sarah your wife shall bear you a son, and you shall call his name Isaac." Abraham could scarcely keep himself from laughing at this announcement. Put yourself in his place: how could he, an old man who had already passed the age when he could be a great-grandfather, still father a child with Sarah, who not only was sterile but had passed the childbearing age? Certainly Abraham, a polygamist (one who has many wives), could still go to one of the women in his harem. But how could such a woman be the mother of the heir promised by God, since God had already excluded Ishmael, the son of the servant Hagar, even though he had otherwise been recognized as Abraham's son.

12 By the oaks of Mamre,
Abraham was visited
by three strangers.
He welcomed them graciously,
asking Sarah to prepare
some fine food.
The strangers,
whom Abraham realized
were messengers of God,
said that Sarah
would soon bear a son.
Unseen, off in a tent,
Sarah heard and laughed.

Noon. It was very hot in the region of Mamre, the high plateau area around Hebron between the Mediterranean and Dead Seas. Fortunately, Abraham had set up camp by a grove of oak trees. And that's where the venerable patriarch was, seated under one of the famous oak trees of Mamre. No doubt he was resting in its shade. Perhaps he was even dozing a bit, because, as the Bible's charming account relates, "he lifted up his eyes and looked, and behold, three men stood in front of him." Instead of addressing all three of them, as one would expect him to, Abraham instead said: "My Lord, if I have found favor in your sight, do not pass by your servant."

Abraham had not made a mistake. It was God whom he was welcoming to his encampment. Quickly, Abraham began preparing to honor his guests and to make them welcome. He called to his wife: "Make three cakes ready quickly and prepare the best milk-fed calf."

As they were feasting on Abraham's food, the guests were wondering: "Where is Sarah?" In Abraham's world, the women did not eat with the men (a custom that is still practiced in certain Muslim countries). Abraham replied to the question by saying, "She is in the tent." And then the Lord said:

> "I will surely return to you in the spring, and Sarah your wife shall have a son." And Sarah was listening at the tent door behind him. Now Abraham and Sarah were old, advanced in age; it had ceased to be with Sarah after the manner of women. So Sarah laughed to herself, saying, "After I have grown old, and my husband is old, shall I have pleasure?" The Lord said to Abraham, "Why did Sarah laugh, and say, 'Shall I indeed bear a child, now that I am old?' Is anything too hard for the Lord? At the appointed time I will return to you, in the spring, and Sarah shall have a son." But Sarah denied, saying, "I did not laugh"; for she was afraid. He said, "No, but you did laugh." (Genesis 18:10-15)

At that point, the three men got up and looked towards the city of Sodom.

13 Abraham and the strangers
went to Sodom,
a city known
for the great evil
that went on there.
God decided to destroy
this city of sin.
Abraham argued with God,
trying to persuade God
not to destroy
any innocent people in Sodom.

The three mysterious persons representing God, whom Abraham had encountered under the oak trees, departed from Mamre and headed towards Sodom, a city to the south of the Dead Sea. Sodom was a city with a burning, dry climate, and Sodom was a city with a terrible reputation. Sodom! — a name in history that people always associate with great evil. Things went on there that cannot even be men-

tioned. For that reason, God decided to destroy this city of sin.

However, Abraham felt compassion for some of the city's inhabitants. He proved himself to be an excellent defender of them. Like an oriental merchant bargaining in the marketplace to get a better price, he pleaded with God on behalf of the righteous, good people in Sodom.

Abraham approached the Lord and asked, "Are you really going to destroy the innocent with the guilty? If there are fifty innocent people in the city, will you destroy the whole city? Won't you spare it in order to save the fifty? Surely you won't kill the innocent with the guilty. That is impossible. The judge of all the earth has to act justly."

The Lord answered, "If I find fifty innocent people in Sodom, I will spare the whole city for their sake."

Abraham spoke again: "Please forgive my boldness in continuing to speak to you, Lord. I am only a man and have no right to say anything. But perhaps there will be only forty-five innocent people instead of fifty. Will you destroy the whole city because there are five too few?"

The Lord answered, "I will not destroy the city if I find forty-five innocent people."

Abraham spoke again: "Perhaps there will be only forty."

He replied, "I will not destroy it if there are forty."

Abraham said, "Please don't be angry, Lord, but I must speak again. What if there are only thirty?"

He said, "I will not do it if I find thirty."

Abraham said, "Please forgive my boldness in continuing to speak to you, Lord. Suppose that only twenty are found?"

He said, "I will not destroy the city if I find twenty."

Abraham said, "Please don't be angry, Lord, and I will speak only once more. What if only ten are found?"

He said, "I will not destroy it if there are ten." After he had finished speaking with Abraham, the Lord went away, and Abraham returned home. (Genesis 18:23-33 TEV)

14 Sodom was so evil
that not even
ten good people
could be found in it,
so Sodom was destroyed.
The family of Lot,
except for Lot's wife,
escaped.
She looked back at Sodom,
even though
warned beforehand
not to do so.

The three mysterious persons who appeared as men of God under the oak trees of Mamre ended up as only two men by the time they reached Sodom, and by then the Bible frankly calls them angels. What happened? A transformation? No, not really. When a writer is telling a story in which symbols are used (something stands for something else), the writer can more freely change details than when telling a true-to-life story. This particular change from three to two persons can also be explained by the fact that at this point several traditions have been woven together into the text of Genesis. However, all these different strands of tradition are

concerned about delivering the same message: God intervenes, or acts, personally in the affairs of human beings.

Two angels, then, arrived at the gates of Sodom. It was evening, cool and fresh compared to the day. Abraham's nephew Lot had watched them approach the city as he sat by the city gate. When the two angels said they wanted

to sleep out all night, Lot insisted that they take shelter in his house. It would have been a violation of the laws of hospitality to allow strangers to sleep outside without shelter. Lot was so insistent that the two angels agreed to accept his hospitality; they entered his house and he served them a meal. But their arrival could not remain unknown in a town the size of Sodom:

Before they lay down, the men of the city, the men of Sodom, both young and old, all the people to the last man, surrounded the house; and they called to Lot, "Where are the men who came to you tonight? Bring them out to us, that we may know them."

(Genesis 19:4-5)

Lot was very upset at the townspeople, who he knew wanted to sexually abuse the strangers, and he cried out to them, "I beg you, my brothers, do not act so wickedly." But the men, burning with passion, simply shouted insults at Lot. They pushed forward against him and tried to break down the door. Fortunately, the two angelic men were watching from inside; they reached out and grabbed Lot and pulled him safely back inside. Then suddenly the mob was struck blind and could not find the door.

This was not the end, however. The two angelic men said to Lot: "God is going to destroy this city. Flee from it with your wife and daughters. Don't look back and don't stop in the valley."

The sun had risen on the earth when Lot came to Zoar. Then the Lord rained on Sodom and Gommorah brimstone and fire out of heaven; and he overthrew those cities, and all the valley, and all the inhabitants of the cities, and what grew on the ground. But Lot's wife behind him looked back, and she became a pillar of salt.   (Genesis 19:23-26)

15 Isaac — son of the promise —
was born
to Abraham and Sarah.
One day while Sarah watched
Isaac and Ishmael playing,
she began worrying that Isaac
might lose out to Ishmael.
She asked Abraham
to banish Hagar and Ishmael.
Hagar and her son
wandered in the desert
until their water was gone.
God told Hagar not to worry,
for her son would live
to begin a great nation.

When the time was ripe and when it pleased God to bring it about, God's promise to Abraham was fulfilled. Sarah bore a son to Abraham. And it was high time, for the old patriarch had just passed his hundredth year. This son, whom his parents had so longed for, they named Isaac, which means "child of laughter."

Ishmael — Abraham's elder son, to whom Hagar had given birth — got along very well with his little brother Isaac. (They were really only half brothers, of course.) One day Sarah came upon the two children playing together. Once more she was upset and fearful that Ishmael might supplant Isaac. She made a scene about it with Abraham, urging that Hagar be sent away. Although Sarah's harsh words displeased Abraham, nevertheless he gave in. Really, though, it was God himself who wanted Abraham to go along with Sarah's proposal:

But God said to Abraham, "Be not displeased because of the lad and because of your slave woman; whatever Sarah says to you, do as she tells you, for through Isaac shall your descendants be named. And I will make a nation of the son of the slave woman also, because he is your offspring." So Abraham rose early in the morning, and took bread and a skin of water, and gave it to Hagar, putting it on her shoulder, along with the child, and sent her away. And she departed, and wandered in the wilderness of Beer-sheba.

When the water in the skin was gone, she cast the child under one of the bushes. Then she went, and sat down over against him a good way off, about the distance of a bowshot; for she said, "Let me not look upon the death of the child." And as she sat over against him, the child lifted up his voice and wept. And God heard the voice of the lad; and the angel of God called to Hagar from heaven, and said to her, "What troubles you, Hagar? Fear not, for God has heard the voice of the lad where he is. Arise, lift up the lad, and hold him fast with your hand; for I will make him a great nation."

(Genesis 21:12-18)

This part of the story seems to be an addition from another tradition. According to the story, Abraham was said to be eighty-six when Ishmael was born, and one hundred at the birth of Isaac. In that case, Ishmael would have had to be fourteen when sent away with his mother; it is difficult to picture his mother putting him down under a bush! This kind of little disagreement shows us again how we must view the Bible as a piece of fabric with different oral traditions woven together.

The Bible tells us that when Ishmael grew up, he became an expert with the bow. His Egyptian mother naturally chose an Egyptian wife for him, and, according to tradition, he lived in encampments and villages in the northern part of Arabia. It is even said that his descendants were organized into twelve groups with twelve chiefs before the fathers of the twelve tribes of Israel were even born.

16 Child sacrifice was customary among the Canaanite people. God asked Abraham to sacrifice his son, Isaac.

The sacrifice of the firstborn child in a family was a custom that was rather widespread in the western part of the ancient Middle East, which included Canaan. Abraham, whose origin was farther east, would have thought it a surprising and cruel custom.

Abraham, however, was always respectful of local customs, just as he always showed himself totally obedient to the voice of God. Whenever God called, Abraham was accustomed to reply, without batting an eye, "Here I am."

In Abraham's case, though, God one day simply commanded Abraham to do a very difficult thing: "Take your son, your only son Isaac, whom you love, and go to the land of Moriah, and offer him there as a burnt offering upon one of the mountains of which I shall tell you."

Abraham must have been astounded at hearing God's strange, difficult command to him. Hadn't he already suffered great anguish about his promised heir? Now that same heir was going to be taken away from him by the very God who had promised him. Was God trying to anger him?

Some Bible scholars think that this incident was actually included in the Bible in order to condemn the practice of child sacrifices. What is certain about the incident, however, is what the Book of Genesis emphasizes about it: The sacrifice was demanded of Abraham because God loved him and was testing his faithfulness. (Later, Jesus would be asked to carry the wood of the cross on which he himself would be sacrificed. The fathers of the Church saw in Isaac's sacrifice a prefiguring, or picturing ahead of time, of the sacrifice of Christ.)

But let us read about this famous incident in the words of the Bible itself:

And Abraham took the wood of the burnt offering, and laid it on Isaac his son; and he took in his hand the fire and the knife. So they went both of them together. And Isaac said to his father Abraham, "My father!" And he said, "Here am I, my son." He said, "Behold the fire and the wood; but where is the lamb for a burnt offering?" Abraham said, "God will provide himself the lamb for a burnt offering, my son." So they went both of them together.

When they came to the place of which God had told him, Abraham built an altar there, and laid the wood in order, and bound Isaac his son, and laid him on the altar, upon the wood. Then Abraham put forth his hand, and took the knife to slay his son. But the angel of the Lord called to him from heaven, and said, "Abraham, Abraham!" And he said, "Here am I." He said, "Do not lay your hand on the lad or do anything to him; for now I know that you fear God, seeing you have not withheld your son, your only son, from me." And Abraham lifted up his eyes and looked, and behold, behind him was a ram, caught in a thicket by his horns;

and Abraham went and took the ram, and offered it up as a burnt offering instead of his son. So Abraham called the name of that place The Lord will provide.

(Genesis 22:6-14)

Then God once again blessed Abraham, saying that Abraham's descendants would be as numerous as the stars in the heavens and the sand on the seashore. And Abraham returned to dwell at Beer-sheba.

17 Abraham sent a servant
to Nahor to find a wife
for his son, Isaac.
Near the town well,
the servant met
a charming and beautiful
young woman
named Rebekah.
He asked for her hand
in marriage for Isaac.

Abraham always was concerned about his descendants. By the time he reached his extreme old age, the marriage of his son Isaac had become his constant worry. So he called in the most faithful servant in his household and charged him with finding a wife for his son in Mesopotamia, the country of his own origin. The servant departed with ten camels laden with gifts.

One fine evening Abraham's servant arrived in Nahor in northern Mesopotamia. He halted with his camels near a well outside the entrance to the town. A charming young girl named Rebekah appeared at the well carrying a water jar upon her shoulder. When Abraham's

servant asked for a drink, she gave him her jar
and also attended to his camels. These gestures
impressed him a great deal, for he had already
prayed to God, "Let the maiden to whom I shall
say, 'Pray let down your jar that I may drink'…
let her be the one whom you have appointed for
your Isaac." Persuaded that the Lord was indicating to him who should be Isaac's bride, the
servant gave Rebekah a gold ring, which he
himself placed in her nostrils, and two gold
bracelets for her wrists.

The servant accompanied Rebekah to her
home, and it turned out that she was none other
than the grandniece of Abraham himself. Her
brother Laban, who was the head of her family,
was happy to offer hospitality to Abraham's
servant.

After much talk, the important moment arrived. Abraham's servant told the entire story
of how his master had entrusted to him the task
of finding among his own kinfolk a bride for
his son, Isaac. Rebekah was asked whether she
would like to go with Abraham's servant, and
she was indeed willing to leave immediately, to
go to the fiancé whom she had not yet seen. At
the moment of parting, Rebekah received this
blessing from her family: "Our sister, be the
mother of thousands of ten thousands." No
doubt her family gazed for a long time at the
caravan that carried Rebekah away towards her
future husband. Meanwhile, back in Canaan,
to the south of Hebron, Isaac waited:

And Isaac went out to meditate in the field in
the evening; and he lifted up his eyes and

looked, and behold, there were camels coming. And Rebekah lifted up her eyes, and
when she saw Isaac, she alighted from the
camel, and said to the servant, "Who is the
man yonder, walking in the field to meet us?"
The servant said, "It is my master." So she
took her veil and covered herself. And the
servant told Isaac all the things that he had
done. Then Isaac brought her into the tent,
and took Rebekah, and she became his wife;
and he loved her. So Isaac was comforted
after his mother's death.   (Genesis 24:63-67)

18 Isaac had two sons:
Esau, who was a hunter
and loved the fields,
and Jacob, who was quiet
and liked to dwell in tents.
One day, Esau was very hungry
and sold his birthright
to Jacob for some lentils.

Rebekah, like her mother-in-law Sarah, at first proved to be sterile. Grieving over this, Isaac prayed to the Lord, "and the Lord granted his prayer and Rebekah his wife conceived." It was after they had been married twenty years that Rebekah presented Isaac with twin boys, very different from each other.

The first came forth red, all his body like a hairy mantle; so they called his name Esau. Afterward his brother came forth, and his hand had taken hold of Esau's heel; so his name was called Jacob. Isaac was sixty years old when she bore them.

When the boys grew up, Esau was a skillful hunter, a man of the field, while Jacob was a quiet man, dwelling in tents. Isaac loved Esau, because he ate of his game; but Rebekah loved Jacob.

Once when Jacob was boiling pottage, Esau came in from the field, and he was famished. And Esau said to Jacob, "Let me eat some of that red pottage, for I am famished!"...Jacob said, "First sell me your birthright." Esau said, "I am about to die; of what use is a birthright to me?" Jacob said, "Swear to me first." So he swore to him, and

sold his birthright to Jacob. Then Jacob gave Esau bread and pottage of lentils, and he ate and drank, and rose and went his way. Thus Esau despised his birthright.

(Genesis 25:25-34)

In this way, Jacob obtained Esau's birthright —the right of an oldest son to inherit his father's goods.

Following this story, the Bible tells another story about Isaac, which begins when he and his family have to depart from the Negev because of famine. Isaac headed for the southern edge of Canaan, to Gerar, that is, to the region that would later be the land of the Philistines. While there, a local king, Abimelech, was taken by the beauty of Rebekah and desired her. He discovered just in time that Rebekah was Isaac's wife.

Isaac knew how to be successful and to achieve prosperity. As the owner of sizable herds, and with a large household, he became an important person in the land. His success aroused jealousy among the local people, especially because he was a foreigner who had simply stopped off to live in their land. One day Isaac found out that someone had filled in the wells that Abraham himself had dug at Beer-sheba in Canaan. This was outrageous. It caused trouble between Isaac's people and Abimelech's people with regard to other local wells. (The Bible frequently speaks about problems concerning wells. Wells were very important for these nomad peoples.)

Isaac, worn down by the conflict, returned to Beer-sheba. And what did he do there? Isaac, like his father Abraham, had more wells dug!

Then, one night when the Lord wished to comfort him, Isaac was blessed with an apparition: He saw God, and his vision reaffirmed the covenant which God had already concluded with Abraham. Meanwhile, by a happy coincidence, Abimelech, from whom Isaac had had to separate because of all the strife over wells, came back to Isaac in friendship because he was convinced of something. He had decided that Isaac's God must be the strongest god because Isaac and his men had proved to be the strongest. And Abimelech therefore wanted to make a covenant with Isaac, whose God was so powerful. It was done, and they feasted over it and exchanged oaths not to fight each other. Then they separated, in peace.

That same day Isaac's servants came and told him about the well which they had dug, and said to him, "We have found water." He called it Shibah; therefore the name of the city is Beer-sheba to this day.

(Genesis 26:32-33)

19 Grown old, Isaac wanted
to bless his successor.
Jacob, with his mother's help,
got the blessing by trickery.
Esau became very angry.

When Isaac felt his death was approaching, he called in Esau for a private talk. At any rate, he thought it was private. However, Rebekah was there, too, able to listen without making any attempt to hide, because by then poor Isaac was blind. He said to Esau:

> "You see that I am old and may die soon. Take your bow and arrows, go out into the country, and kill an animal for me. Cook me some of that tasty food that I like, and bring it to me. After I have eaten it, I will give you my final blessing before I die."
> (Genesis 27:2-4 TEV)

Rebekah, however, preferred her younger son Jacob to her elder son Esau. She wanted Jacob to obtain Isaac's paternal blessing and thus become the heir to the Promise. So she spoke to Jacob, suggesting how she thought they might bring it about. She told Jacob to bring to her two young goats and she would prepare Isaac's favorite dish. Once Isaac ate it, he would be sure to bless Jacob.

But one very serious problem threatened to make the whole plan unworkable:

Jacob said to his mother, "You know that Esau is a hairy man, but I have smooth skin. Perhaps my father will touch me and find out that I am deceiving him; in this way, I will bring a curse on myself instead of a blessing." (Genesis 27:11-12 TEV)

Rebekah replied that he should not let anything like that bother him; she had more than one thing in her bag of tricks. She dressed Jacob in Esau's clothes and covered his hands and neck with the skins of goats. That way Isaac would mistake Jacob for Esau. In fact, that is exactly what happened, although the trick might easily have failed. Isaac, who was

no fool, even remarked that "the voice is Jacob's voice, but the hands are the hands of Esau." However, Isaac did not probe deeply into the reason for this curious fact.

Jacob served his father's favorite dish, which he had brought with him. Smelling the odor of Esau's clothes, Isaac blessed Jacob, remarking that "the smell of my son is as the smell of a field which the Lord has blessed."

When Esau came in from hunting, he cooked some tasty food and took it to his father, saying, "Eat this and give me your blessing."

"Who are you?" Isaac asked.

"Your older son Esau," he answered.

Isaac began to tremble and shake all over, and he asked, "Who was it, then, who killed an animal and brought it to me? I ate it just before you came. I gave him my final blessing, and so it is his forever."

When Esau heard this, he cried out loudly and bitterly and said, "Give me your blessing also, father."

Isaac answered, "Your brother came and deceived me. He has taken away your blessing."

Esau said, "This is the second time that he has cheated me....He took my rights as the firstborn son, and now he has taken away my blessing. Haven't you saved a blessing for me?" (Genesis 27:30-36 TEV)

A blessing was a sacred thing. Once given, it could not be called back. Jacob had gained a very real advantage by cunning and trickery. Since Esau had to get back his position, he was tempted by murderous thoughts against his brother. Rebekah was very aware of Esau's frame of mind, and she was able to warn Jacob in time.

Meanwhile, Esau went to visit their uncle, Ishmael, and married Ishmael's daughter Mahalath—although he already had a Hittite wife, Judith, as well as other wives in his harem. Esau married Ishmael's daughter, a Jewish woman, because he knew his father Isaac did not approve of Canaanite women.

20 Jacob said goodbye to Rebekah. On his way to Haran, he had a dream in which God promised to remain with him.

Jacob, after taking advantage of Esau, had no choice but to say goodbye and leave. He headed towards Haran and the land of the Arameans, the region where his grandfather Abraham had once grazed his flocks after his own departure from Ur.

And he came to a certain place, and stayed there that night, because the sun had set. Taking one of the stones of the place, he put it under his head and lay down in that place to sleep. And he dreamed that there was a ladder set up on earth, and the top of it reached to heaven; and behold, the angels of God were ascending and descending on it."
(Genesis 28:11-12)

This vision of a ladder ascending to heaven was probably influenced by the ancient Mesopotamian temples with their many ascending steps, or even by the Egyptian pyramids. Such a ladder expresses the idea of a link between the Most High God, the Lord above all, and humble people here below.

And behold, the Lord stood above it and said, "I am the Lord, the God of Abraham your father and the God of Isaac; the land on which you lie I will give to you and to your descendants; and your descendants shall be like the dust of the earth, and you shall spread abroad to the west and to the east and to the north and to the south; and by you and your descendants shall all the families of the earth bless themselves. Behold, I am with you and will keep you wherever you go, and will bring you back to this land; for I will not leave you until I have done that of which I have spoken to you." Then Jacob awoke from his sleep and said, "Surely the Lord is in this place; and I did not know it." And he was afraid, and said, "How awesome is this place! This is none other than the house of God, and this is the gate of heaven."

So Jacob rose early in the morning, and he took the stone which he had put under his head and set it up for a pillar and poured oil on the top of it. He called the name of that place Bethel; but the name of the city was Luz at the first. Then Jacob made a vow, saying, "If God will be with me, and will keep me in this way that I go, and will give me bread to eat and clothing to wear, so that I come again to my father's house in peace, then the Lord shall be my God, and this stone, which I have set up for a pillar, shall be God's house; and of all that thou givest me I will give the tenth to thee." (Genesis 28:13-22)

The kind of stone which Jacob set upright is called a *stele*, a stone set up as a boundary marker or monument. Many ancient peoples have erected steles to mark the scenes of battles, victories, and other significant events. Jacob's stone was intended as a memorial to God his protector, to whom Jacob vowed a tenth of his earned wealth, called a *tithe*.

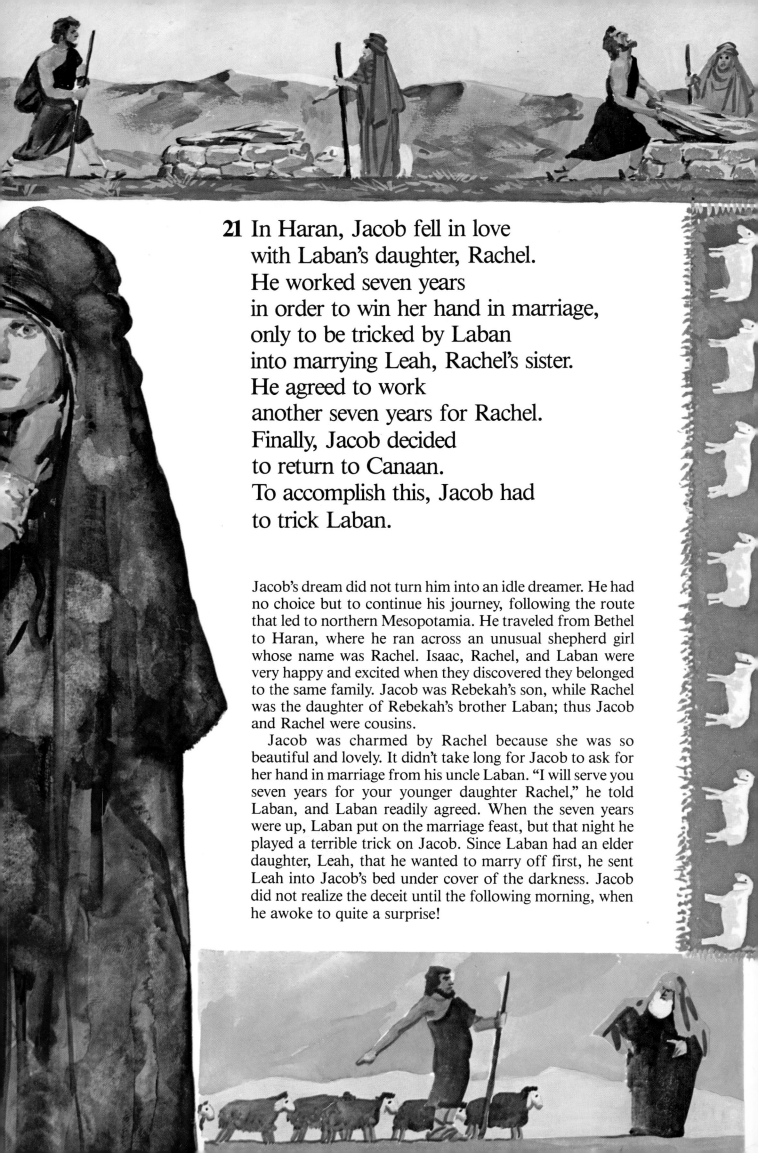

21 In Haran, Jacob fell in love
with Laban's daughter, Rachel.
He worked seven years
in order to win her hand in marriage,
only to be tricked by Laban
into marrying Leah, Rachel's sister.
He agreed to work
another seven years for Rachel.
Finally, Jacob decided
to return to Canaan.
To accomplish this, Jacob had
to trick Laban.

Jacob's dream did not turn him into an idle dreamer. He had no choice but to continue his journey, following the route that led to northern Mesopotamia. He traveled from Bethel to Haran, where he ran across an unusual shepherd girl whose name was Rachel. Isaac, Rachel, and Laban were very happy and excited when they discovered they belonged to the same family. Jacob was Rebekah's son, while Rachel was the daughter of Rebekah's brother Laban; thus Jacob and Rachel were cousins.

Jacob was charmed by Rachel because she was so beautiful and lovely. It didn't take long for Jacob to ask for her hand in marriage from his uncle Laban. "I will serve you seven years for your younger daughter Rachel," he told Laban, and Laban readily agreed. When the seven years were up, Laban put on the marriage feast, but that night he played a terrible trick on Jacob. Since Laban had an elder daughter, Leah, that he wanted to marry off first, he sent Leah into Jacob's bed under cover of the darkness. Jacob did not realize the deceit until the following morning, when he awoke to quite a surprise!

Although Jacob was not pleased by what had been done to him, he was nevertheless obliged to keep Leah as his first wife. First wife? Yes, because in spite of this cruel trick, Jacob didn't give up on his desire to win Rachel. He agreed to work for Laban for seven more years in order to marry Rachel. And he did.

Leah could not help being jealous of Rachel, whom she felt was loved more than she was. Nevertheless she presented Jacob with four healthy sons: Reuben, Simeon, Levi and Judah. Then for a time she became sterile. Just as Sarah had done with Hagar, so Leah gave Jacob her maid Zilpah to bear more children. Zilpah gave Jacob two other sons, Gad and Asher. Then Leah herself gave birth to two more sons, Issachar and Zebulun, and a daughter, Dinah.

Rachel, however, was sterile from the start. She gave her servant Bilhah to Jacob; Bilhah presented Jacob with two sons, Naphtali and Dan. Finally Rachel herself was blessed; she bore Joseph, and, later, as we shall see, Benjamin.

These twelve sons of Jacob gave their names to the twelve tribes of Israel.

Meanwhile, all did not go smoothly between Jacob and Laban. A family quarrel broke out. Once his additional seven years of service to obtain Rachel had been completed, Jacob proposed to Laban the following division of the flocks: Laban would give to Jacob all the spotted and speckled sheep and goats. Laban agreed to this division. But Jacob cheated. He encouraged selective breeding among the flocks so as to produce more spotted and speckled animals. In this way, his own flocks increased enormously.

At this point Jacob was determined to return to his own country with his now teeming flocks, and he decided to leave by night, with all his wives, his sons, and his animals. He was able to leave in good conscience because the Lord had told him in a dream: "Return to the land of your fathers and to your kindred, and I will be with you."

Laban was furious at Jacob for departing like a thief in the night, and he pursued him. He caught up with him in the hill country of Gilead and thoroughly scolded him. Actually, each of them had tried to trick the other in just about equal measure; everything ended with a reconciliation in spite of their differences.

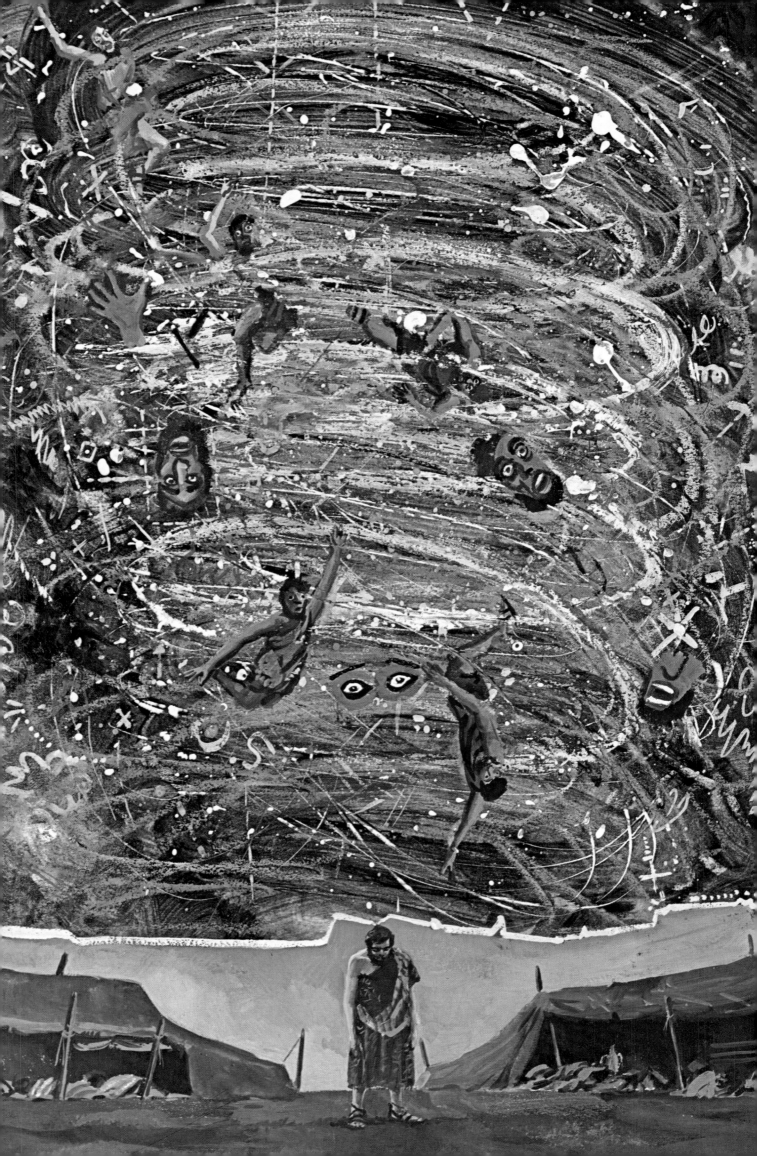

22 On Jacob's journey from Haran,
a mysterious event
changed his life forever.
He wrestled with someone
who gave him
a new name — Israel.
Jacob said he had
seen God face-to-face.
The next day Jacob met Esau.
The brothers made peace, and
Jacob continued his journey.

While he was living in the land of the Arameans, Jacob was far away from his brother Esau. He was also far away from the birthright incident in which he'd cheated Esau with a bowl of lentil stew. But as he approached Canaan on his return journey, Jacob realized he would have to deal with this brother whom he had deprived both of his birthright and blessing. What frame of mind would Esau be in after twenty years of separation? Naturally, Jacob was bringing gifts for him, but what would Esau's reaction be? Jacob was worried.

Finally he reached the Jabbok, a tributary of the Jordan; he sent his wives, children, flock and household across the ford, remaining temporarily alone on the farther side. It was there that a very strange event occurred:

Then a man came and wrestled with him until just before daybreak. When the man saw that he was not winning the struggle, he hit Jacob on the hip, and it was thrown out of joint. The man said, "Let me go, daylight is coming."

"I won't, unless you bless me," Jacob answered.

"What is your name?" the man asked.

"Jacob," he answered.

The man said, "Your name will no longer be Jacob. You have struggled with God and with men, and you have won; so your name will be Israel."

Jacob said, "Now tell me your name."

But he answered, "Why do you want to know my name?" Then he blessed Jacob.

Jacob said, "I have seen God face-to-face, and I am still alive"; so he named the place Peniel. The sun rose as Jacob was leaving Peniel, and he was limping because of his hip. (Genesis 32:24-31 TEV)

This was how Jacob acquired the name *Israel*, the name that was to become the name of the Chosen People and a name that would echo down through history. It means "God struggles," or "he struggles with God." God gave this name to Jacob at the very moment when Jacob was exhibiting the kind of supernatural energy which was going to be required of the whole Chosen People in order for them to fulfill their destiny. Jacob, who was as resourceful as he was cunning, revealed in this incident still another part of his personality: he was a mystic, that is, a person capable of undergoing an experience of God so intense that his or her whole life would be changed. Jacob's meeting with God influenced his meeting with Esau, whom he feared so much.

It was along the route that the brothers met one another. Everything went extremely well. First Jacob sent forward his impressive family — the women first and then the children. Following, he threw himself on the ground before his brother, who ran forward to greet him. The meeting exceeded all Jacob's hopes. The brothers wept with emotion, and they embraced each other. Esau no longer felt angry at Jacob and didn't even scold him.

Still, each brother eventually went his own way. Esau directed his flocks towards Seir, to the south of the Dead Sea, while Jacob moved his on towards Succoth, across the Jordan River.

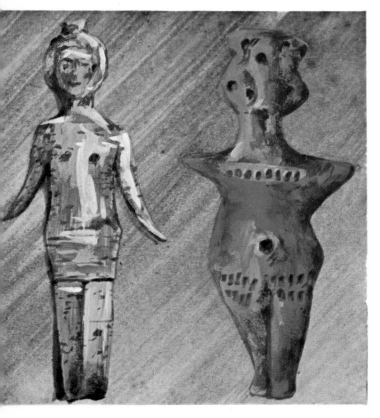

23 God commanded Jacob
to make a pilgrimage
to Bethel. But first,
in order to purify his people,
Jacob ordered the people
to gather all their statues
of household gods and
bury them under a tree.
The caravan then moved
to Bethel to offer sacrifice.
Later, on the way, Rachel
gave birth to Benjamin.

Jacob's sizable caravan passed through the country around both Succoth and Shechem, but, at a certain point, Jacob, responding to a command from the Lord, directed his people towards Bethel:

God said to Jacob, "Arise, go up to Bethel, and dwell there; and make there an altar to the God who appeared to you when you fled from your brother Esau." (Genesis 35:1)

So Jacob gathered together all his household. He gave orders that the little carved idols of pagan gods some of his people carried or wore as earrings must be thrown away. It was not fitting for the faithful of the Lord God Yahweh to be contaminated by the practices of the surrounding pagans. In Mesopotamia, when they were living in Laban's household, it had been difficult to resist becoming attached to these so-called sacred statuettes and jewelry. Even Rachel, when leaving her father's house, had carried off with her some of her father's small household gods, which she had concealed in the pack-saddle of a camel.

Jacob gathered up all these idols and had them buried under a terebinth tree near Shechem. Then he moved to Bethel, where he erected an altar to the Lord. He then called the place El-Bethel, meaning "the God of Bethel," because it was there that God had revealed himself to him when he was fleeing from his brother Esau.

Interwoven with this primarily Yahwist account of Jacob is another account from the priestly source, which tells us something we already know, namely, that Jacob became Israel. This is mentioned in the course of a blessing given by God to Jacob:

God said to him, "Your name is Jacob, but from now on it will be Israel." So God named him Israel. And God said to him, "I am Almighty God. Have many children. Nations will be descended from you, and you will be the ancestor of kings. I will give you the land which I gave to Abraham and to Isaac, and I will also give it to your descendants after you." (Genesis 35:10-12 TEV)

Succoth, Shechem, and Bethel were the principal places where Jacob and his household sojourned. They were moving on to Ephrath when they were forced to halt unexpectedly. Rachel was undergoing a difficult labor, due perhaps to the hardships of the journey. She gave birth to a son in a little village called Bethlehem, but Rachel herself died in childbirth. Her surviving son was Benjamin, which means in Hebrew "the son of the South," or "the son of the right hand." Jacob wept for Rachel even as he rejoiced for Benjamin, his youngest son, born of his beloved Rachel.

Jacob went to his father Isaac at Mamre, near Hebron, where Abraham and Isaac had lived. Isaac lived to be a hundred and eighty years old and died at a ripe old age; and his sons Esau and Jacob buried him.
(Genesis 35:27-29 TEV)

From that time, Jacob established himself permanently in Canaan, in the Hebron Valley.

24 The Book of Genesis tells a series of stories about God's people in the land of Egypt. Over the years, many marvelous events occurred in Egypt, as God guided the Chosen People according to divine plan. The first stories are about Jacob's son, Joseph. Joseph was a wise and forgiving person.

Egypt gave to the world one of the most impressive civilizations of all time. With Egypt are associated the greatest names in the history of the Chosen People: Abraham, Joseph, Moses, and finally, Jesus. Egypt thus deserves to be called a land of the Bible. Let's begin to look now at how this ancient land, Egypt, was involved with the story of Joseph.

Beginning with Joseph, the Book of Genesis recounts a series of stories about marvelous events occurring in the history of God's dealings with his people. The stories are not easy to prove according to the usual rules for writing history. But one thing is certain about these stories, which come from various traditional sources: The stories inspire readers and serve as an example for people because they stress the wisdom of a man who tried to follow God. We admire Joseph for his generosity, while at the same time we approve of his ability to manage things and people and to get things done.

Joseph is certainly a major figure in every respect. He embodies many of the traits that later characterize another Joseph—the foster father of Jesus. He was a just person. Something of God's spirit was revealed in and through him. His heart was not proud, nor did he seek revenge against his brothers. Even though they did him the terrible wrong of casting him into a pit and leaving him for dead, he did no real violence towards them in return.

Nothing indicates, either, that he was ever corrupted by the power that was given to him in Egypt. He resisted the attempts of the wife of the Egyptian officer Potiphar to seduce him. He worked for peace within Egypt as well as for peace with his nomad brothers. He welcomed his brothers with open arms despite the wrong they had done to him, because he remained merciful. Since he himself had been persecuted, he was sympathetic to the plight of others. He was indeed a just person trying to follow the will of God.

All the characteristics Joseph displays in the Old Testament reflect, in fact, God's own wisdom. Without intervening directly in human affairs, God manages to work his will through the good people whom he chooses to act for him. God permits great trials even for those whom he has chosen, because these trials help people on their road to salvation. By saving his brothers from famine, Joseph shows us how all those who hunger and thirst after justice must act. This is one of the main lessons to be learned from the story of Joseph, the man who became the governor of Egypt under Pharaoh.

25 Joseph, who was
his father's favorite son,
had several dreams
about being superior,
in some way,
to his brothers.
His brothers became
jealous and angry,
and when they
had an opportunity,
they plotted
to get rid of Joseph.

Jacob, also known as Israel, had twelve sons. His two youngest sons were Joseph and Benjamin, the children of his beloved Rachel.

Now Israel loved Joseph more than any other of his children, because he was the son of his old age; and he made him a long robe with sleeves. But when his brothers saw that their father loved him more than all his brothers, they hated him, and could not speak peaceably to him.

Now Joseph had a dream, and when he told it to his brothers they only hated him the more. He said to them, "Hear this dream which I have dreamed: behold, we were binding sheaves in the field, and lo, my sheaf arose and stood upright; and behold, your sheaves gathered round it, and bowed down to my sheaf." His brothers said to him, "Are you indeed to reign over us?" So they hated him yet more for his dreams and for his words. Then he dreamed another dream, and told it to his brothers, and said, "Behold, I have dreamed another dream; and behold, the sun, the moon, and eleven stars were bowing down to me." But when he told it to his father and to his brothers, his father rebuked him, and said to him, "What is this dream that you have dreamed? Shall I and your mother and your brothers indeed come to bow ourselves to the ground before you?" And his brothers were jealous of him, but his father kept the saying in mind.

Now his brothers went to pasture their father's flock near Shechem.

(Genesis 37:3-12)

After a while Jacob decided to send Joseph, who had been staying with him, to see how things were going with his brothers. They were pasturing the sheep near Dothan, around twenty miles away from Shechem. Seeing Joseph in the distance, his brothers decided to kill him.

They said to one another: "Here comes this dreamer. Come now, let us kill him and throw him into one of the pits; then we shall say that a wild beast has devoured him, and we shall see what will become of his dreams." But when Reuben heard it, he delivered him out of their hands, saying "Let us not take his life." (Genesis 37:19-21)

The eldest son, Reuben, was unable to go through with killing.

So when Joseph came to his brothers, they stripped him of his robe, the long robe with sleeves that he wore; and they took him and cast him into a pit. (Genesis 37:23-24)

What did poor Joseph think about while he was shivering at the bottom of the pit into which he had been thrown? His brother Judah, who was a little less cruel than his other brothers, proposed a compromise to the others: Instead of shedding their own brother's blood, why not sell him to a caravan of Midianite traders who were headed down to Egypt? Judah's idea was agreed upon, and Joseph was sold to them.

But how would the brothers persuade Jacob that his son was dead? They decided: "We shall make him believe that a wild beast devoured Joseph. Let us slaughter a ram. We will soak his robe in the ram's blood, and take the robe home."

After Jacob heard the story about Joseph, his tears streamed endlessly.

26 In Egypt, Joseph was sold
to an officer named Potiphar.
Joseph resisted
the immoral suggestions
of Potiphar's wife,
but he was unjustly accused
and thrown into prison.
While in prison, Joseph
demonstrated his ability
to interpret dreams.

Joseph was far away in Egypt. The caravan of
Midianite merchants had sold him to one of
Pharaoh's officers, a man named Potiphar.
Potiphar was impressed with Joseph and ended
up putting him in charge of his whole household. Potiphar's wife thought that Joseph was
very handsome. She was so attracted to him
that she even dared to make a proposition to
him: "Lie with me," she said. Joseph always
resisted, and on one occasion turned so quickly

on his heel to get away from her that his coat came off in her hands. Humiliated at Joseph's refusal, Potiphar's wife decided to get back at him. She accused him of having been the one who suggested immoral behavior to her. She used his lost coat in her possession as proof that he had been with her. Punishment was not long in coming, and poor Joseph was thrown into prison.

While Joseph was in prison, two of the other prisoners asked him to interpret dreams of theirs that they had found strange. Joseph agreed to do so. The first man, Pharaoh's chief cup-bearer, told his dream to Joseph:

> So the chief butler told his dream to Joseph, and said to him, "In my dream there was a vine before me, and on the vine there were three branches; as soon as it budded, its blossoms shot forth, and the clusters ripened into grapes. Pharaoh's cup was in my hand; and I took the grapes and pressed them into Pharaoh's cup, and placed the cup in Pharaoh's hand." Then Joseph said to him, "This is its interpretation: the three branches are three days; within three days Pharaoh will lift up your head and restore you to your office; and you shall place Pharaoh's cup in his hand as formerly, when you were his butler. But remember me, when it is well with you, and do me the kindness, I pray you, to make mention of me to Pharaoh, and so get me out of this house. For I was indeed stolen out of the land of the Hebrews; and here also I have done nothing that they should put me into the dungeon." (Genesis 40:9-15)

The second prisoner, Pharaoh's chief baker, then told about a similar strange dream. He had dreamed that he was carrying three baskets of cakes on his head, but that the birds were pecking at the cakes of Pharaoh in the upper-most basket. This was a bad sign. Joseph told him:

> "This is its interpretation: the three baskets are three days; within three days, Pharaoh will lift up your head—from you!—and hang you on a tree; and the birds will eat the flesh from you." (Genesis 40:18-19)

Eventually, the cup-bearer was freed and the baker was executed, just as Joseph had said. The cup-bearer forgot all about Joseph as soon as he was out of prison.

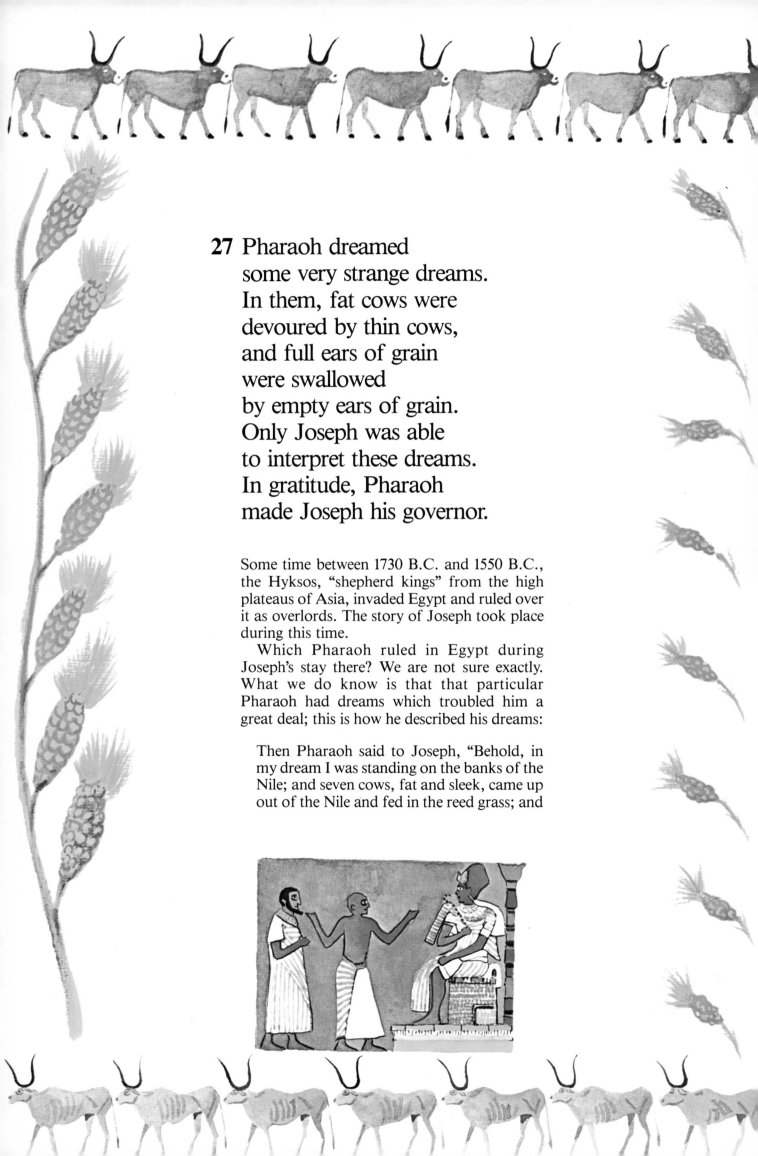

27 Pharaoh dreamed
some very strange dreams.
In them, fat cows were
devoured by thin cows,
and full ears of grain
were swallowed
by empty ears of grain.
Only Joseph was able
to interpret these dreams.
In gratitude, Pharaoh
made Joseph his governor.

Some time between 1730 B.C. and 1550 B.C., the Hyksos, "shepherd kings" from the high plateaus of Asia, invaded Egypt and ruled over it as overlords. The story of Joseph took place during this time.

Which Pharaoh ruled in Egypt during Joseph's stay there? We are not sure exactly. What we do know is that that particular Pharaoh had dreams which troubled him a great deal; this is how he described his dreams:

Then Pharaoh said to Joseph, "Behold, in my dream I was standing on the banks of the Nile; and seven cows, fat and sleek, came up out of the Nile and fed in the reed grass; and

seven other cows came up after them, poor and very gaunt and thin, such as I had never seen in all the land of Egypt. And the thin and gaunt cows ate up the first seven fat cows, but when they had eaten them no one would have known that they had eaten them, for they were still as gaunt as at the beginning. Then I awoke. I also saw in my dream seven ears growing on one stalk, full and good; and seven ears, withered, thin, and blighted by the east wind, sprouted after them, and the thin ears swallowed up the seven good ears. And I told it to the magicians, but there was no one who could explain it to me." (Genesis 41:17-24)

Pharaoh wanted to find someone who could interpret his dreams. It was then that the chief cup-bearer remembered Joseph. Joseph was released from prison and brought before Pharaoh in order to have the contents of the king's dream described to him. Joseph found the dream easy to interpret. He said that God was trying to warn Pharaoh. The seven fat cows and the seven full ears indicated seven years of abundance. The seven gaunt cows and the seven thin ears, however, indicated seven years of famine that would follow. Pharaoh was so impressed by Joseph's wisdom that he soon elevated him to be governor of all Egypt under himself:

And Pharaoh said to Joseph, "Behold, I have set you over all the land of Egypt." Then Pharaoh took his signet ring from his hand and put it on Joseph's hand, and arrayed him in garments of fine linen, and put a gold chain about his neck; and he made him to ride in his second chariot; and they cried before him, "Bow the knee!" Thus he set him over all the land of Egypt. Moreover Pharaoh said to Joseph, "I am Pharaoh, and without your consent no man shall lift hand or foot in all the land of Egypt."

(Genesis 41:41-44)

Pharaoh also gave Asenath, the daughter of Potiphera, to Joseph to be his wife; she was the one who became the mother of Ephraim and Manasseh (later two of the twelve tribal chiefs in Israel).

During the seven years of abundance, Joseph took great care in the management of the country's resources. He saw to it that crops were stored in great abundance so that when the seven years of famine came, Egypt would have plenty stored in its granaries.

28 The famine Joseph predicted
also struck the land of Canaan,
where Jacob still lived.
Jacob sent all his sons,
except Benjamin,
down to Egypt
to buy some grain.
Joseph recognized his brothers
and made them undergo
several tests. Finally,
he sent them home with grain,
keeping Simeon as a hostage.

When the famine actually arrived, Canaan was hit very hard with it. Everyone there considered going down to Egypt, which had become the granary of the Middle East. Jacob himself sent his sons down to try to find grain. He sent all of his sons but one, that is; his youngest son, Benjamin, he kept at home with him. Still suffering from the tragic disappearance of Joseph, Jacob did not want Benjamin, his other son by Rachel, to suffer the same fate as Joseph.

Thus it was that a caravan consisting of ten of Jacob's sons wended its way down to Egypt. The brothers arrived at the palace of Joseph and prostrated themselves before him without recognizing who he was. He, however, as Egypt's governor under Pharaoh, had very good reason to find out the names of all who passed before him. Once he knew just who these men were, however, he had to force himself to deal severely with his brothers. "You are spies," he said to them.

Naturally, his brothers drew together as a family in order to reject such an accusation; they described themselves as being very trustworthy and as coming from a model family: "We, your servants, are twelve brothers, the sons of one man in the land of Canaan; and behold, the youngest is this day with our father, and one is no more." Joseph refused to accept their story; he said that if it was true, then their youngest brother could certainly be brought down to him to prove the story. Then, for good measure, he put his brothers in prison for three days.

After these three days, they were released, but Joseph kept Simeon as a hostage. Very distressed, the brothers said to each other:

"In truth we are guilty concerning our brother, in that we saw the distress of his soul, when he besought us and we would not listen, therefore is this distress come upon us." And Reuben answered them, "Did I not tell you not to sin against the lad? But you would not listen. So now there comes a reckoning for his blood." They did not know that Joseph understood them, for there was an interpreter between them. Then he turned away from them and wept; and he returned to them and spoke to them. And he took

Simeon from them and bound him before their eyes. And Joseph gave orders to fill their bags with grain, and to replace every man's money in his sack, and to give them provisions for the journey. This was done for them.

Then they loaded their asses with their grain, and departed. And as one of them opened his sack to give his ass provender at the lodging place, he saw his money in the mouth of his sack; and he said to his brothers, "My money has been put back; here it is in the mouth of my sack!" At this their hearts failed them, and they turned trembling to one another, saying, "What is this that God has done to us?"

When they came to Jacob their father in the land of Canaan, they told him all that had befallen them.

As they emptied their sacks, behold, every man's bundle of money was in his sack; and when they and their father saw their bundles of money, they were dismayed. And Jacob their father said to them, "You have bereaved me of my children: Joseph is no more, and Simeon is no more, and now you would take Benjamin; all this has come upon me." Then Reuben said to his father, "Slay my two sons if I do not bring him back to you." But he said, "My son shall not go down with you, for his brother is dead, and he only is left. If harm should befall him on the journey that you are to make, you would bring down my gray hairs with sorrow to Sheol."

(Genesis 42:21-29, 35-38)

29 When Jacob's grain was gone,
he told his sons
to return to Egypt.
Jacob let Benjamin go along.
In Egypt, Joseph invited
his brothers to the palace,
and when he saw Benjamin,
he privately wept for joy.
Even so, Joseph gave
his brothers another test.
He had his cup placed
in Benjamin's sack, and
then had Benjamin arrested
for having stolen the cup.

The famine continued. Food became more and more scarce. Everyone looked to Egypt for supplies. Jacob said to his sons, "You must go back." But Judah reminded him that they must not forget the conditions the governor in Egypt had laid down: "Bring your youngest brother to me," he had said. Judah declared that he would guard his brother Benjamin with his own life. Jacob didn't like the situation at all, but ended up agreeing.

Then their father Israel said to them, "If it must be so, then do this: take some of the choice fruits of the land in your bags, and carry down to the man a present, a little balm and a little honey, gum, myrrh, pistachio nuts, and almonds. Take double the money with you; carry back with you the money that was returned in the mouth of your sacks; perhaps it was an oversight. Take also your brother, and arise, go again to the man; may God Almighty grant you mercy before the man, that he may send back your other brother and Benjamin. If I am bereaved of my children, I am bereaved."

(Genesis 43:11-14)

And so for the second time, a caravan of Jacob's set out towards Egypt. As soon as they arrived, they sought out the governor, and bowed and prostrated themselves before him. Once again, Joseph did not let on that he knew them.

And he lifted up his eyes, and saw his brother Benjamin, his mother's son, and said, "Is this your youngest brother, of whom you spoke to me? God be gracious to you, my son!" Then Joseph made haste, for his heart yearned for his brother, and he sought a place to weep. And he entered his chamber and wept there. Then he washed his face and came out; and controlling himself he said, "Let food be served." They served him by himself, and them by themselves, and the Egyptians who ate with him by themselves, because the Egyptians might not eat bread with the Hebrews, for that is an abomination to the Egyptians. (Genesis 43:29-32)

They drank their fill and then took their leave; but they did not go far, for Joseph had arranged still another elaborate trick. He gave orders to the steward of his house:

"Fill the men's sacks with food, as much as they can carry, and put each man's money in the mouth of his sack, and put my cup, the silver cup, in the mouth of the sack of the youngest, with his money for the grain." And

he did as Joseph told him. As soon as the morning was light, the men were sent away with their asses. When they had gone but a short distance from the city, Joseph said to his steward, "Up, follow after the men; and when you overtake them, say to them, 'Why have you returned evil for good? Why have you stolen my silver cup?' " (Genesis 44:1-4)

The steward caught up with the caravan. Panic-stricken, the brothers could not understand what was going on. They solemnly swore that they'd done nothing like what they were accused of. How could they possibly have been so ungrateful as to steal from so generous a prince? The best proof of their innocence, they insisted, was that they had restored the money put into their bags earlier. Would they have done that if they had intended to steal something else?

That remained to be seen. It was decided that the brother found with the silver cup would become a slave. The sacks of grain they were carrying were then quickly brought out and searched, and the governor's silver cup was found in Benjamin's sack.

30 Back in Joseph's presence,
the brothers learned
that Joseph wanted
to keep Benjamin.
Judah offered to take
the place of Benjamin.
Moved by this generous offer,
Joseph revealed his identity.
With joy and love,
the brothers were reunited.

Since the governor's silver cup was found in Benjamin's sack, the caravan of the sons of Jacob was obliged to go back to Egypt to appear before the governor.

"What deed is this that you have done?" Joseph demanded.

And Judah said, "What shall we say to my Lord? What shall we speak? Or how can we clear ourselves? God has found out the guilt of your servants." Judah was obviously referring here to their guilt over what they'd done against Joseph himself.

In this situation, the brothers could do nothing but offer themselves to the governor as slaves. But Joseph refused to accept the offer, indicating that he desired to have Benjamin alone. "Only the man in whose hand the cup was found shall be my slave," Joseph said. "But, as for you, go up in peace to your father."

But Judah pleaded with Joseph: "Now therefore, when I come to your servant my father, and the lad is not with us, he will die; and your servants will bring down the gray hairs of your servant our father with sorrow to Sheol. For your servant became surety for the lad to my father, saying, 'If I do not bring him back to you, then I shall bear the blame in the sight of my father all my life.' "

Then Joseph could not control himself before all those who stood by him; and he cried, "Make every one go out from me." So no one stayed with him when Joseph made himself known to his brothers. And he wept aloud, so that the Egyptians heard it, and the household of Pharaoh heard it. And Joseph said to his brothers, "I am Joseph; is my father still alive?" But his brothers could not answer him, for they were dismayed at his presence.

So Joseph said to his brothers, "Come near to me, I pray you." And they came near. And he said, "I am your brother, Joseph, whom you sold into Egypt. And now do not be distressed, or angry with yourselves, because you sold me here; for God sent me before you to preserve life. Make haste and go up to my father and say to him, 'Thus says your son Joseph, God has made me lord of all Egypt; come down to me, do not tarry; you shall dwell in the land of Goshen, and you shall be near me, you and your children and your children's children, and your flocks, your herds, and all that you have; and there I will provide for you, for there are yet five years of famine to come; lest you and your household, and all that you have, come to poverty.' " Then he fell upon his brother Benjamin's neck and wept; and Benjamin wept upon his neck. And he kissed all his brothers and wept upon them; and after that his brothers talked with him.

(Genesis 44:30-32; 45:1-5, 9-11, 14-15)

31 Back in Canaan, the brothers
told Jacob that Joseph
was still alive.
The entire clan of Jacob
set out for Egypt.
On the way, Jacob and Joseph
had a joyous meeting
in Goshen, the land in which
the Israelites would live
and prosper for many years.

Back in Canaan after their second trip to Egypt, Joseph's brothers told their aged father the incredible news: "The son that you believed dead is alive. He that you thought lost has been found. We have seen him with our own eyes and touched him with our own hands. Joseph is not only alive...he has become the governor of Egypt!" Jacob could hardly believe his ears. It took him awhile to take it all in. But once he had, he said, "I will go and see him before I die."

Joseph had foreseen what would be necessary for the trip which would bring Jacob's entire household down to Egypt. He had furnished his brothers with chariots full of gifts and provisions so that they could bring their father back to Egypt in grand style. This time it was the entire clan of Jacob that set out for the land of plenty—seventy persons in all.

Joseph was watching for Jacob's arrival. As soon as his father's caravan came into view, Joseph harnessed his chariot to ride out to meet him. The meeting of the father and son, who had both given up hope of ever seeing each other again, was an emotional reunion, with many hugs and many tears. Then it was time to present Joseph's family to Pharaoh:

The king asked them, "What is your occupation?"

"We are shepherds, sir, just as our ancestors were," they answered. "We have come to live in this country, because in the land of Canaan the famine is so severe that there is no pasture for our flocks. Please give us permission to live in the region of Goshen." Then Joseph settled his father and his brothers in Egypt, giving them property in the best of the land near the city of Rameses, as the king had commanded.

(Genesis 47:3-4, 11 TEV)

Jacob lived in Egypt for seventeen years. Then, weary and feeling his 147 years, he became ill. He called together his sons and gave each of them a personal blessing. To Joseph, he said:

"Blessings of grain and flowers,
Blessings of ancient mountains,
Delightful things from everlasting hills.
May these blessings rest
    on the head of Joseph,
On the brow of the one set apart
    from his brothers."   (Genesis 49:26 TEV)

When Jacob had finished blessing his twelve sons, he gave some instructions for his burial. Then he lay back down and died.

Joseph and his brothers did as Jacob had requested. They took his body to Canaan and buried it in the burial ground of his ancestors.

Eventually Joseph also died. He was embalmed and placed in a coffin in Egypt, and many years later his family took his body to be buried in Canaan.

As the Book of Genesis ends, the Israelites are still living in Egypt. The Bible continues its history of the Chosen People with the story of Moses.

Reuben Simeon Judah Zebulon Issacher Dan Gad Asher Naphtali Ephraim Manasseh Benjamin

32 The Nile River made Egypt rich.
Each year its floods left
good soil, ready for planting.
People from drier lands nearby
often came to Egypt to stay.
Jacob's family came and stayed
for four hundred years.
While they were there,
Egyptians made them slaves.

The people who called themselves "the sons of Israel"—and whom others called "the Hebrews"—experienced many changes once they had left the shepherd's way of life of their father Jacob. No longer did they live as nomads, as they had in Canaan; now instead they led a settled life in the eastern part of the Nile delta.

The land of Egypt is called "the gift of the Nile," and that's a good name for it. Egypt's fertile soil is not watered by rain; it practically never rains there. Rather, each year the Nile overflows and floods its river valley, depositing a rich, fertile layer of mud before retiring back within its banks and thus leaving the soil ready for planting.

More than once in the days of the pharaohs, semi-desert nomads would move up to the edge of the fertile part of Egypt, driven there by seasonal droughts, by famine, or by the drying up of their usual pastures. Sometimes the officers of the Egyptian frontier guards would allow such nomads to remain. Undoubtedly this is what happened in the case of Jacob and his sons when they arrived in Egypt with their wives, children, slaves, and numerous animals.

Around 1700 B.C., northern Egypt had been conquered by a people from the north, from

Syria, called *the Hyksos*, that is, "the chiefs of foreign lands." They built heavy fortifications around the small towns that dotted Canaan. They also introduced from Asia Minor — then the country of the Hittites — the use of horses and war chariots, which had been unknown in Egypt up until then. Through their military strength, the Hyksos were able to take over the government of Egypt. They established their capital at Avaris in the Nile delta, and, from there, they extended their rule over northern Egypt and also into Canaan. It is easy to understand how a ruling family in Egypt that was itself foreign would have welcomed other foreigners such as the Israelites, and would have allowed them to settle down in the land of Goshen, east of the delta.

How long did the Israelites stay in Egypt? It's likely that they were there for as long as four hundred years. During this time, their population increased enormously, and they became a numerous people.

During these four hundred years, there were many changes within Egypt, too. Around 1570 B.C., the Pharaoh Ahmose I expelled the Hyksos and pushed them beyond the frontiers of Egypt. Then the Egyptians themselves began to make conquests, especially under Pharaoh Thutmose III, who conquered both Canaan and Syria.

These lands were still under Egypt's control during the long reign of Rameses II, who ruled from about 1300 B.C. to 1240 B.C. Rameses was forced to fight off the Hittites of Asia Minor, who had invaded the Egyptian possessions in Syria. Consequently, Rameses greatly needed many workers to build and furnish towns along the Egyptian frontier which could house his soldiers. Since he needed help in the area where the Israelites had settled, Rameses made slaves of the descendants of Jacob's sons. They weren't used to this kind of labor, of course, having been mostly shepherds, who prized their own freedom of movement. Now they had to face the fact that they were no longer guests in Egypt, more or less tolerated by the authorities; instead they had become the slaves of the Egyptians.

It was at this time, during the reign of Rameses II, that Moses was born.

33 Egypt had a long history even before the patriarchs.
The pharaoh, or ruler, had unlimited power.
Egyptians worshiped many different gods of nature.

Rameses II (son of Seti I, who had inaugurated the nineteenth dynasty) had to struggle with the Hittites of Asia for control of these northern Egyptian possessions. He eventually

When Moses was born under the Pharaoh Rameses II, Egypt already had an ancient history. Over fifteen hundred years before Moses, the kings of the first Egyptian dynasty had united the two previously independent parts of the land. These first dynasty kings then began calling themselves "the kings of Upper and Lower Egypt."

The pharaohs strongly believed that the entire Nile River had to be controlled under a single government, for the sake of the rich agriculture in the Nile Valley. Egypt's history under the pharaohs is usually divided into three successive periods: 1. There was the Old Kingdom, with its capital at Memphis (in the North), which lasted up until about 2700 B.C.; this was the period when the great pyramids were built. 2. Then there was the Middle Kingdom. Its capital was at Thebes (in the South). 3. Finally, there was the New Kingdom, which began with the eighteenth dynasty, which expelled the Hyksos around 1570 B.C. This dynasty also conquered Canaan and Syria, countries that remained under Egyptian domination for about four hundred years.

signed an agreement with them that fixed the borders of Egypt's possessions in northern Syria. In order to oversee his northern possessions more efficiently, Rameses set up a residence at Tanis in the Nile delta. He lived in a new town called "the House of Rameses," which was constructed by the Israelite slaves.

The power of the Egyptian pharaohs—the word *pharaoh* means "the great house"—was unlimited and absolute. In fact, the pharaoh was considered a divinity, or god. He was the sole owner of the nation's entire territory—except for the temples, which were considered to belong to the gods. Under the pharaohs there were usually one or two national governors, or viceroys, as well as provincial governors, military chiefs and court officials.

Most of the Egyptian people worked in agriculture. Egyptian artisans achieved very high quality work in figurative art as well as in the production of both luxury objects and objects for everyday use. There was also a class of scribes, to which most government officials belonged; the scribes studied the ancient temple writings and composed new ones; they wrote poems and maxims (short sayings) of practical wisdom, including proverbs similar to those found in the Bible.

Egyptian religion honored the gods Amon of Thebes and Ra (or Re) of Heliopolis, both of which were sun gods. Osiris was the god of the world of the dead, as well as the god of agriculture. His sister (and wife) was the goddess Isis; his son was Horus, who was believed to have been the first king to reign in Egypt. Each pharaoh was thought to be a reincarnation of Horus.

Other divinities were represented by means of animal heads. The cult of these animal-gods became more and more popular in Egypt, especially in the New Kingdom and after, because people thought the animal-gods possessed special divine powers.

Egyptian religion taught people certain magical practices intended to insure a happy survival in the next world. One such practice involved embalming dead bodies and placing all kinds of objects in tombs of the dead.

Towards the end of the eighteenth dynasty, around 1370-1350 B.C., the Pharaoh Amenhotep IV, also called Ikhnaton, tried to impose a new religion upon ancient Egypt. Ikhnaton believed in one god, manifested in the sun, or solar disk. However, Ihknaton's attempt to establish monotheism (a belief in and worship of one god) was abolished by the priests of Thebes and by his successor, the Pharaoh Tutankhamen.

34 Angry, the Pharaoh made the Israelites gather their own straw for making bricks.

Rameses II, the absolute king of the New Kingdom in Egypt, was the greatest builder among the pharaohs. His glory was reflected in all its splendor in his colossal temple at Abu Simbel. He also built new towns — Pithom and Raamses, market cities northeast of the delta.

In order to carry out his building projects, Rameses needed plenty of cheap laborers. He found these laborers at hand in the Hebrews, the name given by the Egyptians to the sons of

And the Egyptians were in dread of the people of Israel. So they made the people of Israel serve with rigor, and made their lives bitter with hard service, in mortar and brick, and in all kinds of work in the field; in all their work they made them serve with rigor. (Exodus 1:9-14)

The Hebrews' situation grew worse when Moses and Aaron (about whom we'll learn much more later) asked Pharaoh to let the Hebrew people make a three-day pilgrimage into the desert to worship God.

This request provoked Pharaoh into making life even harder for the Israelites:

The same day Pharaoh commanded the taskmasters of the people and their foremen, "You shall no longer give the people straw to make bricks, as heretofore; let them go and gather straw for themselves. But the number of bricks which they made heretofore you shall lay upon them, you shall by no means lessen it; for they are idle.

So the people were scattered abroad throughout all the land of Egypt, to gather stubble for straw. The taskmasters were urgent, saying, "Complete your work, your daily task, as when there was straw." And the foremen of the people of Israel, whom Pharaoh's taskmasters had set over them, were beaten, and were asked, "Why have you not done all your task of making bricks today, as hitherto?" (Exodus 5:6-8, 12-14)

Israel living in the land of Goshen. The Hebrew people had never really been assimilated into the Egyptian population. They had their own customs and religion. Also, their population had grown steadily over the years, disturbing the Pharaoh.

And he said to his people, "Behold the people of Israel are too many and too mighty for us. Come, let us deal shrewdly with them, lest they multiply, and, if war befall us, they join our enemies and fight against us and escape from the land." Therefore they set taskmasters over them to afflict them with heavy burdens; and they built for Pharaoh store-cities, Pithom and Raamses. But the more they were oppressed, the more they multiplied and the more they spread abroad.

35 Afraid that there were
too many Israelites,
the Egyptians tried to kill
all Hebrew baby boys.
Moses was saved,
and was raised
by the family of Pharaoh.
One day Moses in anger
killed an Egyptian
who was overseeing
the Hebrew slaves.

Exodus. The word comes from the Greek and it means "a going out." This name is given to the second book of the Bible because this book tells how Israel "went out" of Egypt, discarding the yoke of its slavery.

This "good news" about a people who passed from slavery into freedom is told in the language of wonders and miracles. Throughout Israel's entire history, the people's fabulous passage through the Sea of Reeds and across the desert would be told and retold in order to bear witness to God's great act of liberating this people. It is important to emphasize the event's meaning: The people did not free themselves; God liberated them. It was God who decided, alone, to renew the covenant with the Israelites, just as God had originated the covenant with Abraham.

Generation after generation of Israelites interpreted the Exodus as God's great "saving event" in the history of the Chosen People. It was the decisive event of their history; all their religious practices and rites referred back to it. Generation after generation saw that this "sacred history" required a great act of faith: "Who is this Lord who cannot be seen but with whom we have a covenant? What is God's name? Why does God put us to the test?"

Finally, this "saving event" of the people of God, Israel, recalls the major event of Christianity, Jesus' Resurrection, which, like the Exodus, also involves a people's passage from bondage to freedom. The passage that we made as a result of Jesus' death and his Resurrection takes us out of the slavery, or the shadows, of sin into the freedom, or light, of Christ.

The Book of Exodus consists of traditional stories written down around the fifth century B.C. It is the second of the first five biblical books, commoly known as "The Pentateuch." (In Greek, *penta* means "five.") These five books form the Hebrew "Torah," or "Law." The Book of Exodus begins with Moses' birth.

The years when Joseph was the governor of Egypt were long past. The reigning pharaoh

had become worried about the steady growth of the Israelite population. Perhaps the Israelites might even supplant the Egyptians themselves. Not satisfied with having subjected the Hebrews to forced labor, Pharaoh now ordered that any newborn Hebrew boys should be put to death.

One day, however, a Hebrew woman of the tribe of Levi gave birth to a healthy baby boy. Since she couldn't bear to think of the baby boy's being killed, she tried to save him by putting him in a papyrus basket lined with pitch and then setting the basket, with its precious cargo, afloat among the reeds that lined the banks of the Nile.

Soon the daughter of Pharaoh passed by. Seeing the basket, she uncovered the crying baby inside, and her heart went out to him. She decided to adopt the baby. And as a wet-nurse for him, she hired none other than the baby's own mother.

The baby's name was Moses, which means "saved from the water." Raised at Pharaoh's court, Moses received an excellent Egyptian education. But he never forgot that he was a Hebrew by birth. Once, while visiting his people hard at work, he witnessed an Egyptian overseer striking a Hebrew. Angered by this injustice, Moses ended up killing the overseer.

36 After killing the Egyptian,
Moses fled, to save his life.
He settled in Midian,
part of Arabia.
There he worked for Jethro,
a shepherd, and married
one of his daughters.
Once while watching the flock,
he saw a strange sight,
a bush that was on fire,
but was not burned.

Pharaoh learned about Moses killing the overseer, and so he sought to have Moses killed. Moses fled in fear to the land of Midian, a region inhabited by nomads in northwest Arabia, southwest of Edom and extending to the port of Elath along the coast facing the Sinai peninsula.

One day, seated near a well, Moses saw the daughters of Jethro, a priest of Midian, coming to water their flocks at the well. Soon other shepherds arrived and chased the women away. Moses immediately defended the women and made sure they were able to water their flocks.

As soon as Jethro's daughters returned home, they told their father about the day's events and how Moses had helped them. "Go find the man," Jethro said, "and invite him to come and eat with us." They did so, and Moses ended up becoming one of Jethro's herdsmen and marrying one of his daughters, Zipporah. (She became the mother of Moses' first son, Gershom, meaning "a sojourner" or "immigrant.")

Meanwhile, things were not getting any better for the Israelites back in Goshen. In fact, they were getting worse. The Israelites were calling on God to help them in their plight. God heard them and realized how miserable they were.

At this point, the Bible relates how God manifested himself to one of his people. This theophany is perhaps the best known in the entire Bible. It is the time, on Mount Horeb (or Sinai), that God appeared to Moses in a burning bush:

Now Moses was keeping the flock of his father-in-law, Jethro, the priest of Midian; and he led his flock to the west side of the wilderness, and came to Horeb, the mountain of God. And the angel of the Lord appeared to him in a flame of fire out of the midst of a bush; and he looked, and lo, the bush was burning, yet it was not consumed. And Moses said, "I will turn aside and see this great sight, why the bush is not burnt." (Exodus 3:1-3)

37 From the bush, Moses heard God calling him to lead Israel out of Egypt to the Promised Land.

Moses had not gotten over his surprise at seeing a bush burning without being consumed, when he heard a voice speaking to him from out of the flames. It was indeed God who was speaking to him:

> "I have seen the affliction of my people who are in Egypt, and have heard their cry because of their taskmasters; I know their sufferings, and I have come down to deliver them out of the hand of the Egyptians, and to bring them up out of that land to a good and broad land, a land flowing with milk and honey, to the place of the Canaanites, the Hittites, the Amorites, the Perizzites, the Hivites, and the Jebusites. And now, behold, the cry of the people of Israel has come to me, and I have seen the oppression with which the Egyptians oppress them. Come, I will send you to Pharaoh that you may bring forth my people, the sons of Israel, out of Egypt." (Exodus 3:7-10)

Moses was simply overcome by this revelation. He said, "Who am I that I should go to Pharaoh and bring the children of Israel out of Egypt?" Just as the prophet Jeremiah also would do later on, Moses hesitated mightily before attempting to take on such a mission — even though the mission had been given to him by God. God had to urge and encourage him. "I will be with you," God told Moses.

Then Moses said to God, "If I come to the people of Israel and say to them, 'The God of your fathers has sent me to you,' and they ask me, 'What is his name?' what shall I say to them?" God said to Moses, "I AM WHO I AM." And he said, "Say this to the people of Israel, 'I AM has sent me to you.'" (Exodus 3:13-14)

Moses felt that to be accepted by the people, he needed proofs. Just as Jacob, wrestling with God at Jabbok, wanted to know God's name, so now Moses made the same demand. God is a "hidden God," as the Bible says, yet at the same

time God speaks to us in a unique way that is clear even while it remains obscure. God reveals himself and at the same time holds back. God makes himself known, and at the same time God's identity remains veiled. God is a paradox, that is, God contains what seems like contradictions to us.

What does the name Yahweh mean? It is an unusual Hebrew word with four consonants—YHWH—that was translated "I am who I am," or, as scholars prefer to translate it today, "I will be who I will be." The use of the future verb tense conveys the idea that God is open to infinite possibilities. "You haven't really discovered everything about me," God seems to be saying. "You see only what you can see."

However, this mysterious name of Yahweh seems to have another, very real meaning. Remember that the gods of the Canaanites and Babylonians did not really exist. ("They have... eyes, but do not see. They have ears, but do not hear," as one psalm expresses it.) But the God of Abraham, of Isaac, and of Jacob really did and does exist; this God says "I am" for the simple reason *that he is*! Moses learns a single name of a single and unique God, nothing like the Babylonian god Marduk, who had fifty or so different names.

The Lord. This is the way Yahweh was referred to whenever anyone spoke about or to him. And for a very simple reason: To call someone by his or her name, according to the ancient Hebrews, was to acquire a power over that person. However, no one can really acquire any power over God or take advantage of God. That is why in all the different periods of time covered by the Old Testament the people always found another name to use for God. In the time of the patriarchs, God was called *El Shaddai*, a name that means "the God of the mountains," or "the Most High." Only later did the Hebrews speak of the Lord, or God, or the Lord God. But these are all names given to a being whom we cannot understand fully.

It is in this way that God maintains, at the same time, both great freedom and unmeasureable mystery. Once again, we know God as a paradox: near to us, while at the same time at an infinite distance from us. Near, because God does speak to people; far away, because people can come near only at God's invitation. God's distance from us is shown in the command to Moses, "Do not come near; put off your shoes from your feet, for the place on which you are standing is holy ground."

38 Moses was slow to answer
God's call, but finally Moses,
with his brother Aaron, said yes.
They went to Pharaoh
and demanded a few days
of freedom for a feast
of worship in the desert.

already had it done, for the rite was certainly practiced in Egypt.)

Moses continued on his way and met Aaron in the desert, as the Lord had said he would. The two brothers embraced.

Afterwards the two brothers went to Pharaoh and said, "The Lord, the God of Israel says, 'Let my people go that they may hold a feast to me in the wilderness.'"

But Pharaoh—many believe he was the Pharaoh Rameses II—had been enoying using

Even though God had assured Moses that he would be with him to help lead the Israelites out of Egypt, Moses still hesitated. He was afraid. "They will never believe me!" he thought.

As a sign of Moses' authority, therefore, God brought about a miracle. God changed a rod into a serpent and the serpent back into a rod. But even that marvel did not seem to be enough to convince Moses. He was still unsure of himself. So God said to him, "Is there not Aaron, your brother, the Levite? He is a very convincing speaker. He shall speak for you to the people."

Moses then returned to Midian, to the household of Jethro, gathered his wife and sons, and set out for Egypt. On the way, something important occurred, although it remains mysterious:

Zipporah took a flint and cut off her son's foreskin, and touched Moses' feet with it, and said, "Surely you are a bridegroom of blood to me!" Then it was that she said, "You are a bridegroom of blood," because of the circumcision. (Exodus 4:25-26)

It was important that the son of the Israelites' leader should be circumcised. From the time of Abraham, this rite was the sign of the covenant with God. (It's puzzling why Moses had not

the Israelites as a source of cheap labor, and he was not about to let them go. Why should he? Not only would the output of bricks be diminished, but there was another risk. Give an enslaved people such as the Hebrews three days away from their brickyards, and Pharaoh would probably never see them again. Celebrating a "feast" to God in the wilderness might be merely an excuse to flee. Though Pharaoh said no to Moses and Aaron, the Lord told them to persist:

"If the king demands that you prove yourselves by performing a miracle, tell Aaron to take his walking stick and throw it down in front of the king, and it will turn into a snake." So Moses and Aaron went to the king and did as the Lord had commanded. Aaron threw his walking stick down in front of the king and his officers, and it turned into a snake. Then the king called for his wise men and magicians, and by their magic they did the same thing. They threw down their walking sticks, and the sticks turned into snakes. But Aaron's stick swallowed theirs. The king, however, remained stubborn and, just as the Lord had said, the king would not listen to Moses and Aaron.

(Exodus 7:9-13 TEV)

39

Pharaoh was stubborn
and refused to let
the Israelites go.
According to the Bible,
God punished the Egyptians
severely with plagues,
such as hailstorms,
swarms of locusts, and
the Nile River
turning red with blood.

Pharaoh continued to refuse the Israelites permission to leave. As a consequence, a series of misfortunes came upon Egypt. Epidemics and other catastrophes fell upon the country with such violence that, even though they were generally related to events in nature, they appeared to be extraordinary. At any rate, they were certainly interpreted as scourges inflicted upon Egypt as punishment for Pharaoh's stubbornness.

Egypt suffered ten plagues in all: water changed into blood; an invasion of frogs; clouds of mosquitoes, or gnats; swarms of flies; plagues among the Egyptians' animals; outbreaks of boils; hailstorms; swarms of locusts; darkness over the earth; and the deaths of all the firstborn of the Egyptians. Here are a few examples from the Bible:

The Lord said to Moses, "Tell Aaron to take his stick and hold it out over all the rivers, canals, and pools in Egypt. The water will become blood, and all over the land there will be blood, even in the wooden tubs and stone jars."

Then Moses and Aaron did as the Lord commanded. In the presence of the king and his officers, Aaron raised his stick and struck the surface of the river, and all the water in it was turned into blood. The fish in the river died, and it smelled so bad that the Egyptians could not drink from it. There was blood everywhere in Egypt. Then the king's magi-

cians did the same thing by means of their magic, and the king was as stubborn as ever. Just as the Lord had said, the king refused to listen to Moses and Aaron.

(Exodus 7:19-22 TEV)

The rod was the same one the Lord had once changed into a serpent. The serpent was the emblem of Pharaoh's power. In changing it back into a rod, Moses was demonstrating the power of the God who worked through him—and this power was superior to that of Pharaoh.

Then the Lord said to Moses and Aaron, "Take a few handfuls of ashes from a furnace; Moses is to throw them into the air in front of the king. They will spread out like fine dust over all the land of Egypt, and everywhere they will produce boils that become open sores on the people and the animals." (Exodus 9:8-9 TEV)

Boils did, in fact, cover them. In the case of this plague and all the others it was God's power that showed itself.

And the Lord turned a very strong west wind, which lifted the locusts and drove them into the Red Sea; not a single locust was left in all the country of Egypt. But the Lord hardened Pharaoh's heart, and he did not let the children of Israel go. (Exodus 10:19-20)

The accounts of all these plagues are fearful stories. The Yahwist and priestly sources both contributed to the stories, and all together the stories present a thorough examination of the problem of evil. Pharaoh is frequently presented as responsible for his own hardness of heart; at other times, God is represented as prompting Pharaoh to this hardening. What is the truth? Is Pharaoh really free and responsible? Why does he persist in not letting the Israelites go? Sometimes the Bible simply does not answer the questions that it raises.

What seems clear here, though, is that we are dealing with signs and wonders intended to throw light on the idea of a Savior-God. The Israelites were destined to be liberated—but only after a high price was paid.

40 God passed over the Israelites and struck dead the firstborn of the Egyptian people.

One plague after another occurred. But nothing stopped Pharaoh. Pharaoh remained stubborn, refusing to let the children of Israel go. So it came about that the Lord had to take really strong action. The God whose name was Yahweh, "I am Who I am," was about to deliver his people from Egypt.

What God wanted the Jews to do next was laid out in detail for them:

Tell all the congregation of Israel that on the tenth day of this month they shall take every man a lamb according to their fathers' houses, a lamb for a household; and if the household is too small for a lamb, then a man and his neighbor next to his house shall take according to the number of persons; according to what each can eat you shall make your count for the lamb....The whole assembly of the congregation of Israel shall kill their lambs in the evening. Then they shall take some of the blood, and put it on the two doorposts and the lintel of the houses in which they eat them. They shall eat the flesh that night, roasted; with unleavened bread and bitter herbs they shall eat it.

(Exodus 12:3-4, 6-8)

The Lord warned that his passing through the land would be terrible for the Egyptians:

For I will pass through the land of Egypt, that night, and I will smite all the first-born in the land of Egypt, both man and beast; and on all the gods of Egypt I will execute judgments: I am the Lord. The blood shall be a sign for you, upon the houses where you are; and when I see the blood, I will pass over you, and no plague shall fall upon you to destroy you when I smite the land of Egypt. (Exodus 12:12-13)

At midnight, the Lord passed over the land of Egypt, and all the firstborn of the Egyptians were killed, even the Pharaoh's son. There was great weeping in every house. This was the Passover of the Lord.

41 Pharaoh told the Israelites
to leave but then changed
his mind and pursued them.
Moses stretched out his arm,
and the people passed unharmed
through the Sea of Reeds.

Pharaoh summoned Moses and Aaron and said, "Leave at once, you and your people! Go! Worship the Lord as you wish."

So after living for more than four hundred years in Egypt, the Israelites prepared to return to Canaan, the land promised by God to the patriarchs, to Abraham, Isaac, and Jacob.

We don't know the exact date of their departure from Egypt. However, we are reasonably sure that the Exodus took place during the last years of the Pharaoh Rameses II, around 1240 B.C. to 1230 B.C., or during the first years of the reign of his successor, Meneptah.

We also don't know exactly how many Israelites there were who went out of Egypt. But certainly there were thousands of them.

However many there were, after the Passover of the Lord, they journeyed from Raamses to Succoth. From the eastern frontier of Egypt, they headed south toward the caravan route that led across the Sinai Desert, and they set up camp near the Sea of Reeds.

(Although the Bible text says they went to the Red Sea, the correct translation is really "Sea of Reeds" or "Reed Sea.")

Meanwhile, the Egyptians regretted having allowed the Israelites to leave. So they gathered a great force — Pharaoh's whole army, his horses, chariots, and chariot drivers, the Bible says — and set off to recapture the Israelites.

The Israelites were terrified at the thought of pursuit. Unlike the Egyptians, they were not trained for war. They did not even have any weapons, and, besides, they had their wives, children, and animals with them. They knew they would be defeated in any battle, so when they spotted Pharaoh's army drawing near, they cried in fright to Moses, "Why did you do this? Why did you bring us out to die in the desert?"

Moses asked the Lord what to do, and the Lord said to Moses,

> "Why are you crying out for help? Tell the people to move forward. Lift up your walking stick and hold it out over the sea. The water will divide, and the Israelites will be able to walk through the sea on dry ground."
> (Exodus 14:15-16 TEV)

God did indeed act to protect his people, just as on the night of the Passover. Both the Yahwist and the priestly traditions tell us what happened:

> Then Moses stretched out his hand over the sea; and the Lord drove the sea back by a strong east wind all night, and made the sea dry land, and the waters were divided. And the people of Israel went into the midst of the sea on dry ground, the waters being a wall to them on their right hand and on their left.
> (Exodus 14:21-22)

Once again, God had liberated his people. This is the significance of the people's passage through the waters of the Reed Sea, even though we don't know exactly how it all came about.

The passage from slavery to freedom would not be merely a human accomplishment; it would be a manifestation of God's saving power. The Jews would come to regard the Exodus from Egypt as God's crucial saving act in their history. It would be celebrated as a ritual of liberation throughout the history of the Jews.

Christians also recall the Passover and Exodus when they celebrate Easter. The New Testament writers use the Exodus and the events associated with it to describe the life, death, and resurrection of Jesus.

Each year when the Jews celebrate the Passover, they are marking the anniversary of their liberation. The entire biblical tradition looks back to the great events of the Exodus, so much so that the Exodus is considered the true "founding event" of the people of Israel. Not only that, but God became known primarily as the God who had delivered the Israelites from slavery in Egypt. God even addressed them as such: "I am the Lord your God, who brought you out of the land of Egypt, out of the house of bondage."

I will sing to the Lord
for he has triumphed gloriously;
the horse and his rider
he has thrown into the sea.
The Lord is my strength and my song,
and he has become my salvation.

(Exodus 15:1-2)

42 The Egyptians—soldiers,
chariots, and chariot drivers—
raced after the Israelites.
When the Egyptians were
in the midst of the sea,
Moses stretched out his arm,
and the waters flowed back.
Not a single Egyptian escaped!
God had saved his people.
The Israelites celebrated this event
in the Song of Moses.

For when the horses of Pharaoh with his chariots and his horsemen went into the sea, the Lord brought back the waters of the sea upon them; but the people of Israel walked on dry ground in the midst of the sea. Then Miriam, the prophetess, the sister of Aaron, took a timbrel in her hand; and all the women went out after her with timbrels and dancing. And Miriam sang to them:
"Sing to the Lord,
    for he has triumphed gloriously;
    the horse and his rider he has thrown
        into the sea."

(Exodus 15:19-21)

Pharaoh's chariots and his host
    he cast into the sea;
    and his picked officers are sunk
        in the Red Sea.
The floods cover them;
    they went down into the depths
        like a stone.
Who is like thee, O Lord, among the gods?

(Exodus 15:4-6, 11)

43 The Israelites headed toward Canaan, the Promised Land. There were three ways to cross the Sinai Desert. The Israelites likely followed the western route.

Zoar

Pithom

After the passage through the Reed Sea, the Israelites had to undergo the ordeal of the desert. Crossing a desert is never easy. In the desert, a straight line is not necessarily the shortest distance between two points; it is also necessary to take into account the location of existing wells or springs, of trails, and of suitable campsites. At the time of Moses, there existed three possible routes that could be followed on the journey to Canaan.

The northern route. Later this would be called the Way of the Philistines. It followed the shore of the Mediterranean Sea, and was the most direct route to Canaan. It is certainly logical to think the Hebrews might have chosen this one, except that the main event during their sojourn in the desert was their stop at Mount Sinai; and this Mediterranean route does not go that way. Also, if we remember that the Hebrews were fleeing from Pharaoh, then we realize that they would not have taken this

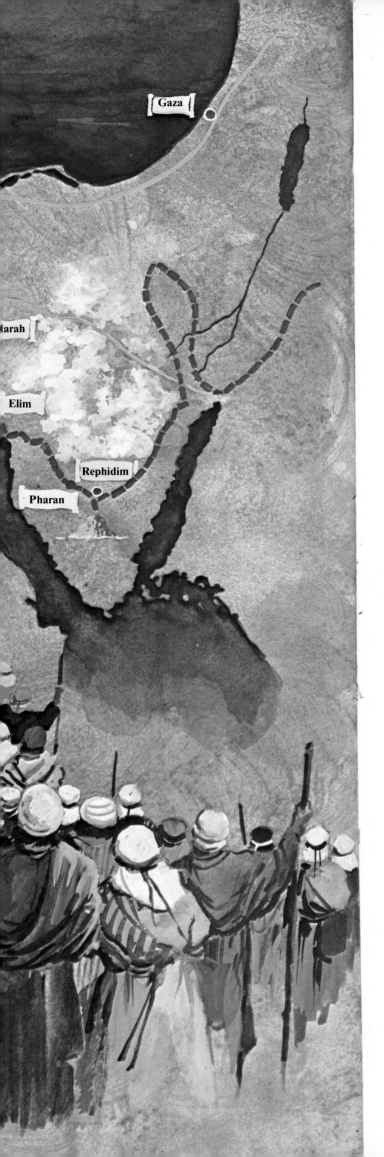

route because it was a major route for Egypt, with Egyptian military outposts all the way along it. The Israelites would have been stopped immediately, and so it is quite unlikely that they would have walked right into this danger.

The central route. This route was called the caravan route. It cut the Sinai peninsula neatly in half. However, it would not have been an easy route to follow for any caravan weighed down with families and household goods. Since there were no wells or suitable campsites along it, caravans were forced to pass right through.

Many people hold that the camel was not yet domesticated at the time of Moses, and hence it would have been impossible to carry any large supply of water for the crossing. Yet the distance involved required three days to cross. Usually only the nomad spice merchants who traveled between Arabia and Canaan managed to take this route, and they traveled light.

It is difficult to imagine how the people that followed Moses out of Egypt could have managed this route. Probably they used another route.

The western route. This route was called the turquoise route because it was used by the miners who extracted this precious stone for Pharaoh, just as they extracted copper, in the region of Serabit el Khadim. This route led south from the Sea of Reeds towards the Sinai peninsula. It is in this general direction that modern archeologists and scholars tend to locate some of the places made famous by their being mentioned in the Book of Exodus and in sacred tradition. Worth mentioning, moving from north to south, are the following:

Ayn Muse. This is an oasis today called "the fountains of Moses." In the Bible, it is called Elim, and it had, the Bible says, "twelve springs of water and seventy palm trees."

Marah. This is where the Hebrews found the water unfit to drink—bitter, like their own plight.

Old Pharan. This was at the foot of Mount Serbal. Today it is called the Wadi Pheran, and it is a marvelous oasis with its palm and acacia trees.

Rephidim. It was here, according to sacred tradition, that Moses struck the rock, and water gushed out. Moses called it Massah ("the test") and Meribah ("the quarreling") because the people found fault with the Lord, demanding proof that he was truly with them.

The existence of such sites as these seems to indicate that this western route was the one Moses followed.

44 In the desert the Israelites,
worn out with hunger,
complained and thought about
returning to Egypt.
The Lord intervened again.
First, God sent quail
that could easily be hunted.
Then, God sent manna,
a special kind of bread.
Still many Israelites
were not satisfied.

The march in the desert was not easy for the Israelites. Worn out and weakened by hunger and thirst, Moses' band began to cry out, "Who will give us food to eat?"

"We remember the fish we ate in Egypt for nothing, the cucumbers, the melons, the leeks, the onions, and the garlic; but now our strength is dried up, and there is nothing at all but manna to look at." (Numbers 11:5-6)

Indeed, the Lord had made a strange kind of dew rain down upon them.

And when the dew had gone up, there was on the face of the wilderness a fine, flakelike thing, fine as hoarfrost on the ground. When the people of Israel saw it, they said to one another, "What is it?" For they did not know what it was. And Moses said to them, "It is the bread which the Lord has given you to eat."

Manna was like small seeds, whitish yellow in color. It fell on the camp at night

along with the dew. The next morning the people would go around and gather it, grind it or pound it into flour, and then boil it and make it into flat cakes. It tasted like bread baked with olive oil.

(Exodus 16:14-15; Numbers 11:7-9 TEV)

Over the years, many people have speculated about just what this miraculous food was. One theory says that manna was the leaves or foliage of certain bushes. Another theory claims it was a sweet pitch, or gum, produced by the tamarisk trees that are found in the Sinai Desert. Depending upon how we look at it, manna can also be considered a poor excuse for real food, intended to teach the lesson that people do not live by bread alone but by gratitude to the God who gives it. But who can say for sure what manna was? We don't really know any more about it now than the Hebrews in the desert when they asked, "What is this?"

What is clear, though, is that the Hebrews became dissatisfied with it and asked for meat.

And there went forth a wind from the Lord, and it brought quails from the sea, and let them fall beside the camp, about a day's journey on this side and a day's journey on the other side, round about the camp, and about two cubits above the face of the earth. And the people rose all that day, and all night, and all the next day, and gathered the quails; he who gathered least gathered ten homers; and they spread them out for themselves all around the camp. While the meat was yet between their teeth, before it was consumed, the anger of the Lord was kindled against the people, and the Lord smote the people with a very great plague. Therefore the name of that place was called Kibrothhattaavah, because there they buried the people who had the craving.

(Numbers 11:31-34)

Because the people refused to accept with gratitude the manna, the food provided by God, the Lord sent an epidemic as punishment.

45 At Rephidim,
the Israelites repelled
the attack of the Amalekites
through the intercession
of Moses.
After this danger was past,
Jethro arrived with Zipporah.
It was a happy reunion.
Jethro suggested to Moses
that he appoint judges
to help him rule
the people of Israel.

Week after week the Israelites toiled on their march through the desert. How long did it take them? It isn't possible to say exactly, but we know they had to pass through miles and miles of arid land dotted with sparse desert bushes and grasses. How many people even remained out of the many Hebrew tribes that had followed Moses out of the land of Goshen? They had certainly undergone many ordeals since their departure from Egypt: hunger, thirst, and epidemics, as well as roving robbers, who attacked desert nomads. The Amalekites, chief people in the Negev desert, fought with them:

The Amalekites came and attacked the Israelites at Rephidim. Moses said to Joshua, "Pick out some men to go and fight the Amalekites tomorrow. I will stand on top of

the hill holding the stick that God told me to carry." Joshua did as Moses commanded him and went out to fight the Amalekites, while Moses, Aaron, and Hur went up to the top of the hill. As long as Moses held up his arms, the Israelites won but when he put his arms down, the Amalekites started winning. When Moses' arms grew tired, Aaron and Hur brought a stone for him to sit on, while they stood beside him and held up his arms, holding them steady until the sun went down. In this way Joshua totally defeated the Amalekites.   (Exodus 17:8-13 TEV)

But there were not just enemies in the desert; there were also friends. There was Jethro, for instance, the father-in-law of Moses, who lived in the land of Midian on the other side of Sinai. Word of his son-in-law's exploits had reached Jethro, and he came to meet Moses in Sinai, accompanied by Zipporah and Moses' two sons, Gershom and Eliezer. Moses told Jethro about all the things he had been able to accomplish — thanks to God's help. Then Jethro himself made a great profession of faith in God: "Blessed be the Lord, who has delivered you out of the hands of the Egyptians and out of the hand of Pharaoh," Jethro said. "Now I know that the Lord is greater than all the gods."

Jethro participated with Moses in a burnt offering and sacrifice offered to God. Then the two men along with Aaron and all the elders of Israel shared a meal in which they ate some meat from the animals that were sacrificed.

After this, the daily life of the camp went on. Before long, Jethro noticed that Moses was occupied from morning to night judging the disputes and differences that arose among the people of Israel. Jethro felt this work was too much for Moses alone. "You are not able to perform this alone," he said. "Find other men to help you, and you be the chief judge." Moses heeded his father-in-law's advice and chose a number of men to be over different groups and clans of the people: "And they judged the people at all times; hard cases they brought to Moses, but any small matters they decided themselves."

This is how Moses happened to begin the practice of appointing wise men who later would be known as "the judges" over Israel.

Jethro said goodbye to Moses and returned to his home in Midian.

46 The Chosen People arrived at the slopes of Mount Sinai, where God's glory was revealed through thunder and lightning. Moses ascended Mount Sinai, and it was there that the covenant was sealed between God and the Israelites.

With the chiefs under Moses acting as "judges" over each group or clan, the community led by Moses seemed to be both well-organized and solidly established. They had set up camp at the base of a massive crystalline mountain range in the southern part of the Sinai peninsula. These mountains contained one of humankind's most sacred spots—Mount Sinai.

Whenever Mount Sinai is mentioned, it is Moses who first comes to mind. The Arabs even call the mountain Jebel Musa, meaning "Mount Moses." It is also known as Mount Horeb, the Holy Mountain, or the Fire Mountain, about which one speaks with "fear and trembling" since it was there that the earth trembled, as Psalm 68 tells us.

It was on Mount Sinai that Moses witnessed the burning bush and found himself face-to-face with God. It was there also that he would receive the Ten Commandments, just as, later, the prophet Elijah would meet the Lord there. From the beginning of the Christian era, anchorites, or solitary monks, would establish themselves in the same desolate area, and, in the eleventh century, the famous Monastery of

Saint Catherine would be built on the mountainside there. Today thousands of pilgrims still visit this remote spot every year, seeking to put their feet on the same ground that Moses walked on.

It was while the children of Israel were camping at the foot of Mount Sinai, three months after their exodus from Egypt, that the Lord called Moses to come up on the mountain in order to make a covenant with him:

And the Lord said to Moses, "Go to the people and consecrate them today and tomorrow, and let them wash their garments, and be ready by the third day; for on the third day the Lord will come down upon Mount Sinai in the sight of all the people. And you shall set bounds for the people round about, saying, 'Take heed that you do not go up into the mountain or touch the border of it; whoever touches the mountain shall be put to death.' " On the morning of the third day there were thunders and lightnings, and a thick cloud upon the mountain, and a very loud trumpet blast, so that all the people who were in the camp trembled. And as the sound of the trumpet grew louder and louder, Moses spoke, and God answered him in thunder. (Exodus 19:10-12, 16, 19)

It was then that God revealed the Ten Commandments, or Decalogue. This list of prohibited acts recalls similar lists that were found in ancient Babylon, as well as others in ancient Egypt. Long before the time of Moses, in the reign of the Pharaoh Amenemhet III (nineteenth century B.C.), a stele was inscribed listing some forbidden acts. After the time of Moses, the Egyptians were still inscribing such stones; one discovered at Abydos, for example, has the Pharaoh Rameses IV confessing:

"I did not eat what was forbidden to me.
I did not kill the innocent.
I did not steal from the poor."

The Pharaoh's claims of innocence to the god Osiris display a standard of behavior similar to the Decalogue of Moses. Many scholars today study how different religions have influenced one another.

47 God gave to Moses the tables of the law containing the Ten Commandments, or Decalogue.

You shall have no other gods before me. You shall not make any idol or graven image or bow down before them.

Honor your father and your mother.

You shall not take the name of the Lord your God in vain.

You shall not kill.

Remember the sabbath day to keep it holy.

You shall not commit adultery.

You shall not covet your neighbor's house.

You shall not steal.

You shall not covet anything that belongs to your neighbor.

You shall not bear false witness against your neighbor.

48 The Chosen People did not have
only the Ten Commandments
to guide them.
They developed
other, more detailed laws
for daily living.
Because the Israelites
remembered how God
had rescued them from slavery,
their laws stressed love for
the poor, the weak, widows,
orphans, and strangers.

The Ten Commandments make up the heart of
the law that God revealed to Moses on Mount
Sinai. The Decalogue is the creed of Israel, the
foundation of the laws developed by the people
of God. The laws, in turn, emphasize helping
the poorest of outcasts and the disinherited:

> "You shall not wrong a stranger or oppress
> him, for you were strangers in the land of
> Egypt. You shall not afflict any widow or or-
> phan. If you do afflict them, and they cry out
> to me, I will surely hear their cry; and my
> wrath will burn, and I will kill you with the
> sword, and your wives shall become widows
> and your children fatherless.
>
> If ever you take your neighbor's garment
> in pledge, you shall restore it to him before
> the sun goes down; for that is his only cover-
> ing, it is his mantle for his body; in what else
> shall he sleep? And if he cries to me, I will
> hear, for I am compassionate.
> (Exodus 22:21-24, 26-27)

The Israelite laws went into great detail, and
regulated the conduct of the people down to the
slightest acts in the course of their daily life.
Here is only one example:
> "When an ox gores a man or a woman to
> death, the ox shall be stoned, and its flesh
> shall not be eaten; but the owner of the ox
> shall be clear. But if the ox has been ac-
> customed to gore in the past, and its owner
> has been warned but has not kept it in, and it
> kills a man or a woman, the ox shall be
> stoned, and its owner also shall be put to
> death." (Exodus 21:28-29)

Thus, out of the Ten Commandments grew
the laws of the covenant, which governed the
social and religious life of the people.

In the centuries that followed Moses, the
Israelites always called Moses their great law-
giver. He was the one who had delivered to
them the basic law revealed by God — the Ten
Commandments.

But Moses did not actually write down the
entire body of laws flowing from the Ten Commandments. That occurred over many years,
while the Israelites were gradually becoming a
settled people; it became final in the seventh
century B.C. In 622 B.C. the Israelite King
Josiah discovered a book which contained an
old, forgotten version of Israelite laws. Josiah
ordered a review and reform of these laws and,
when corrected, the laws became the biblical
Book of Deuteronomy (a word which means
"the second law").

The Book of Deuteronomy invited the people to live good, upright lives in recognition of
God's gift of the covenant. Above all, their
observing God's commandments expressed
their faithfulness to a God whose law can also
be summed up in a single word — love. These
words of the Lord are the great revelation in the
Book of Deuteronomy:

> "Hear, O Israel: the Lord our God is one
> Lord; and you shall love the Lord your God
> with all your heart, and with all your soul,
> and with all your might. And these words
> which I command you this day shall be upon
> your heart." (Deuteronomy 6:4-6)

Much later, when Jesus became angry at
some of the Pharisees, it was because they had
forgotten something very important about the
law. These doctors of the law were so busy
trying to carry out the details of Jewish law that
they forgot the spirit which gives life to it — love.

49 The people were afraid
that Moses would not return
from the mountain top.
So Aaron made a golden calf
which they worshiped as a god.
When Moses came down
from the mountain,
he broke the tables of the law
and punished the guilty ones.
Then he went back
up the mountain
to renew the covenant.

Life had become very monotonous for the Israelites in the desert. Moses had been gone for forty days and forty nights, absent on Mount Sinai. The people felt abandoned and believed they would never see him again, so they began to have some forbidden thoughts. An invisible God was a nice idea, they thought; but they wanted some way in which to represent God so that they could celebrate his worship, just as the Egyptians celebrated the worship of their gods. One day, therefore, they said to Aaron:

"We do not know what has happened to this man Moses, who led us out of Egypt; so make us a god to lead us."

Aaron said to them, "Take off the gold earrings which your wives, your sons, and your daughters are wearing, and bring them to me." (Exodus 32:1-2 TEV)

Aaron melted down all the gold he received and out of it he fashioned a statue of a calf. He then built an altar in front of the golden calf and declared, "Tomorrow shall be a feast to the Lord." The next day, everyone feasted and danced.

In making this golden calf at the people's request, Aaron and the people were not necessarily proposing to dethrone the true God, to abandon the Lord. From the inscriptions on some Babylonian steles, we know that the calf was considered as a symbol of strength and fertility and sometimes was used as a pedestal for statues of gods. The Israelites' golden calf may

calf. My wrath may burn hot against them and I may consume them. But I will still make a great nation of you." Just as happened in the time of Abraham, God wanted to desert this people and start all over again. But Moses interceded with God for his people just as Abraham had done. "Lord, do not treat them thus," Moses responded. "If you do, the Egyptians will believe you brought them out of Egypt merely in order to have the pleasure of slaying them in the wilderness."

have been tied up with such an idea, or suggested by it. Maybe in erecting a calf the people intended only to make a visible sign of the presence of the invisible God.

Nevertheless, this act of the children of Israel was very questionable, since it is so easy to forget the invisible God behind the representation. The act of making the calf was, therefore, a sinful one—a betrayal of the covenant.

Thus the Lord had to warn Moses: "Go down, quickly. Your people are a stiff-necked race. They are bowing down before a golden

Having said this, Moses came down from the holy mountain in a fury at his people. When he saw the golden calf, he was so enraged that he broke the tables of the law carved in stone that he had brought down with him from Mount Sinai. He burnt the golden calf and then ground it down to powder. He scolded Aaron, guilty of having yielded to the wicked demands of a people gone astray.

Then Moses called out: "Who is on the Lord's side? Come to me." The sons of Levi, the members of the tribe to which he himself belonged, rallied around him; and Moses ordered them in God's name to slay others in the camp for what they'd done. More than three thousand were put to the sword. After this massacre, Moses again ascended Mount Sinai to plead for those who had been spared. The Lord finally forgave Israel for being unfaithful to the covenant.

50 Here are pictured the main
objects used in Hebrew worship:
in the center,
the ark of the covenant
with two cherubim above it;
on the left,
the table of the presence
and the basin for washing;
on the right,
the altar of burnt offering,
the altar of incense,
and the seven-branched
candlestick.

After having revealed his law, the Lord also
made known the manner in which he was to be
worshiped in the desert. The objects that the
Israelites used in worship were listed precisely in
the Torah.

A special tent was set aside as a sanctuary, a
holy place dedicated to the worship of God.
This sanctuary, called the tabernacle, housed
the ark of the covenant. The tabernacle containing the ark, together with the sacred ground
around it, was the place where God was to be
consulted in order to learn divine revelations.
Moses met God there alone in order to receive
his orders. Later, the Temple in Jerusalem
would take the place of this tent in the desert;
both were the sanctuary, or dwelling-place, of
God.

The dwelling-place of God! The tabernacle
was a tent composed of several layers. The first,
inner layer was of red linen set within a frame
of acacia wood plated with gold and set up on
bases made of silver. This first tent was covered
with another made of goat-hair, which in turn
was covered with layers of ram and goat skins.
The tent's entrance was covered by a curtain,
and inside, it was separated into two parts by a
veil decorated with skillfully-worked cherubim.

"The holy" contained the table of the presence, with twelve loaves of unleavened bread as symbols of God's covenant with the twelve tribes; the seven-branched Jewish candlestick (called a menorah) made of pure gold; and the altar of incense. "The holy of holies" contained the ark of the covenant.

The arc of the covenant was a chest made of acacia wood, roughly a cubic yard in volume. It contained the tablets of the law. Four golden rings were fixed along its sides through which poles could be passed so that it could be carried like a stretcher. Above the ark there was a sort of covering called a "mercy seat." Two golden cherubim facing each other were mounted above the ark, with their outspread wings overshadowing it. The space between these wings was the empty space signifying God's invisible presence. Temples similar to the Israelite tabernacle can be found, for example, at Edfu, in Egypt, where there is a boat, or "bark for eternity," supporting two cherubim with outspread wings. It is difficult to determine which religion influenced which.

Outside the sacred tent were the altar of acacia wood, where animals were burnt in sacrifice to God, and the bronze basin, where the priests washed.

We must picture this sacred place, established with such ornate care and richness, as being in the barren desert. And the question arises as to how desert nomads in Sinai obtained all the materials necessary for such elaborate worship. Acacia wood was certainly plentiful enough in such spots as the oasis of the Wadi Feiran. But gold, silver, and bronze? How could the Israelites have melted down all these metals? How did they obtain items such as curtains or goat skins? Or get tools to use for construction? How could they have managed all this when they were forced to struggle for just a bare living in the desert?

Common-sense questions such as these are answered when we remember that the Bible's accounts of the Hebrews' desert worship were only actually written down centuries later, after the time of Solomon and the construction of the Temple. Some of the Temple's grandeur was attached to the Hebrews' worship during the time of Moses.

51 During the time of Moses,
formal worship was established
among the Israelites.
Aaron, Moses' brother, was ordained
as the first high priest.
On the left, Aaron is being dressed
in the sacred robes.
On the right, sacrifices are being offered
at Aaron's consecration.
In the center are pictured
the special garments worn
by the high priest.

During the time of the patriarchs, the Hebrews had no formal liturgical worship conducted by priests. (Liturgical worship is official public worship always carried out in the same set way.) Not until Moses' time were the priesthood and liturgical worship established among the Israelites. One day the Lord said to Moses: "Bring near to you Aaron your brother, and his sons with him, from among the people of Israel, to serve me as priests."

It was by God's order that Aaron, at age eighty-five, was ordained as the first high priest. The liturgy of consecration of priests had three parts: being dressed in sacred robes, or vestments; being anointed; and offering sacrifices.

The description in the Book of Exodus of all the sacred ornaments and vestments no doubt refers to practices occurring much later than Moses' time. It probably really describes the luxurious worship practices of the Temple at Jerusalem. At that time it was certainly easier to procure all the rare cloths and precious accessories in which Aaron and the other priests were supposed to be clothed.

A priest wore a purple outer robe; around the bottom were little bells interspersed with embroidered pomegranates. Underneath, he wore linen underclothing covering the loins down to the thighs. Over all, he wore a linen outer apron called an "ephod," which was held on with suspenders. The ephod was embroidered with gold and had two onyx stones on which were engraved the names of the sons of Israel (Jacob).

A priest also wore a breastplate, a kind of square pouch inlaid with four rows of beautiful precious jewels. This breastplate contained the Urim and Thummim, which were sacred lots (objects used in trying to foresee and know fate, or destiny). What they were exactly is not well understood.

In addition to all this, the priest wore a tunic and a linen turban; the turban had a gold plate on it, inscribed with the words "Holy to the Lord." This gold plate was the sign of priesthood that each priest received at the moment he was anointed with holy oils.

Then the sacrifice took place at the entrance to the tent. A young bull was killed and its blood spread around the base of the altar. Then first one ram and then another were slaughtered and burned upon the altar. The blood of the second ram was used to anoint various parts of the priest's body. When the sacrifice was finished, the flesh of the rams was eaten.

This was the way a son of Aaron the Levite became a priest from the time of Moses on, even in the desert. From Psalm 119, we learn how marvelous it was to be a priest:

Blessed are those whose way is blameless,
   who walk in the law of the Lord!
Blessed are those who keep his testimonies,
   who seek him with their whole heart,
who also do no wrong,
   but walk in his ways!
Thou hast commanded thy precepts
   to be kept diligently.
O that my ways may be steadfast
   in keeping thy statutes!
Then I shall not be put to shame,
   having my eyes fixed on all thy commandments.
I will praise thee with an upright heart,
   when I learn thy righteous ordinances.
I will observe thy statutes;
   O forsake me not utterly!   (Psalm 119:1-8)

52 To the Chosen People,
the people of the covenant,
God was to provide
a Promised Land.
Moses was the mediator
of the covenant.
He spoke to the people
to remind them
of the obligations
that were part of
their covenant with God.
He also interceded with God
to ask pardon
for his unfaithful people.

The Israelites remained for a long time around Mount Sinai, although we do not know exactly how long. At a certain point, though, God came to Moses and said:

"Depart, go up hence, you and the people you have brought up out of the land of Egypt. Go up to a land flowing with milk and honey." (Exodus 33:1, 3)

God described what the Promised Land would be like:

"For the land which you are entering to take possession of it is not like the land of Egypt, from which you have come, where you sowed your seed and watered it with your feet, like a garden of vegetables; but the land which you are going over to possess is a land of hills and valleys, which drinks water by the rain from heaven, a land which the Lord your God cares for; the eyes of the Lord your God are always upon it, from the beginning of the year to the end of the year.

"And if you will obey my commandments which I command you this day, to love the Lord your God, and to serve him with all your heart and with all your soul, he will give the rain for your land in its season, the early rain and the later rain, that you may gather in your grain and your wine and your oil. And he will give grass in your fields for your cattle, and you shall eat and be full.

(Deuteronomy 11:10-15)

However, because the people had been sinful and unfaithful in the desert, God did not wish to accompany them:

The Lord had commanded Moses to tell them, "You are a stubborn people. If I were to go with you even for a moment, I would completely destroy you. Now take off your jewelry, and I will decide what to do with you." So after they left Mount Sinai, the people of Israel no longer wore jewelry.

(Exodus 33:5-6 TEV)

(The Lord commanded that the people discard their remaining jewelry because jewelry had been used in the construction of the golden calf.)

It was in this sad state that the Israelites set out once again. And, once again, they experienced problems and crises on their journey. For example, on one occasion, at Hazeroth, Aaron and his sister Miriam spoke out against Moses because of Moses' second wife, an Ethiopian woman. The Lord became angry at them because they dared to criticize Moses, the leader chosen by the Lord. And so Miriam was afflicted with leprosy. She was cured only through the goodness of Moses, who interceded once again with the Lord. Meanwhile the people headed towards the wilderness of Paran.

53 Scouts sent by Moses found Canaan to be rich, but well-defended. Fearful, the people rebelled against Moses.

After a ten-day march across the wilderness of Paran, the Israelites reached Kadesh, a large oasis containing lands with scrub bushes and some palm trees. A spring flowed amid reeds, feeding a number of pools lined with trees. In fact, the oasis contained several small springs, thus permitting people to settle for a time. It was there that the Israelites camped for a lengthy period. (Miriam died during this stopover.)

From this oasis, a patrol was sent to spy out the land of Canaan. God said to Moses: "Send men to spy out the land of Canaan, which I give to the people of Israel." Joshua and Caleb were among those who went on this mission. The spies passed through the wilderness of Zin, through the Negev desert, and up as far as Hebron. In the Valley of Eshkil, they obtained a cluster of grapes, which they took with them when they reported back to Moses:

And they told him, "We came to the land to which you sent us; it flows with milk and honey, and this is its fruit. Yet the people who dwell in the land are strong, and the cities are fortified and very large; and besides, we saw

the descendants of Anak there. The Amalekites dwell in the land of the Negeb; the Hittites, the Jebusites, and the Amorites dwell in the hill country; and the Canaanites dwell by the sea, and along the Jordan."

But Caleb quieted the people before Moses, and said, "Let us go up at once, and occupy it; for we are well able to overcome it." Then the men who had gone up with him said, "We are not able to go up against the people; for they are stronger than we." So they brought to the people of Israel an evil report of the land which they had spied out, saying, "The land, through which we have gone, to spy it out, is a land that devours its inhabitants; and all the people that we saw in it are men of great stature.

(Numbers 13:27-32)

Hearing this, the people revolted against the idea of occupying Canaan. They protested loudly against Moses and Aaron, weeping and blaming them. "We should have died in Egypt," they cried. "Would it not be better for us to go back to Egypt? Let us choose a captain and go back to Egypt."

Then Moses and Aaron bowed to the ground in front of all the people. And Joshua son of Nun and Caleb son of Jephunneh, two of the spies, tore their clothes in sorrow and said to the people, "The land we explored is an excellent land. If the Lord is pleased with us, he will take us there and give us that rich and fertile land. Do not rebel against the Lord and don't be afraid of the people who live there. We will conquer them easily. The Lord is with us and has defeated the gods who protected them; so don't be afraid." The whole community was threatening to stone them to death, but suddenly the people saw the dazzling light of the Lord's presence appear over the Tent.

The Lord said to Moses, "How much longer will these people reject me? How much longer will they refuse to trust in me, even though I have performed so many miracles among them? I will send an epidemic and destroy them, but I will make you the father of a nation that is larger and more powerful than they are!"

(Numbers 14:5-12 TEV)

Once again, Moses had to intercede for the people. And once again the Lord pardoned them, but this time he laid down a restriction: None of the people who rejected the Lord would ever be allowed to enter the Promised Land.

54 When drinking water grew
scarce in the wilderness,
Moses caused water to gush
out of a rock.
Eleazar succeeded his father
Aaron as high priest.
Poisonous serpents
infested the camp;
Moses set up a bronze serpent,
which cured anyone
who looked upon it in faith.

Did the springs at Kadesh run dry? Certainly drinking water grew very scarce, according to the Bible. Because of this, the angry people revolted against the leadership of Moses and Aaron. The Yahwist tradition claims this revolt over drinking water occurred at Kadesh. The priestly version locates it at Rephidim just before the Israelites plunged into Sinai. Wherever it happened, Moses and Aaron, faced with revolt, went to the entrance of the sacred tent and threw themselves down on the ground there. The glory of the Lord appeared to them and told them to strike the rock for water.

And Moses and Aaron gathered the assembly together before the rock, and he said to them, "Hear now, you rebels; shall we bring forth water for you out of this rock?" And Moses lifted up his hand and struck the rock with his rod twice; and water came forth abundantly, and the congregation drank, and their cattle.   (Numbers 20:10-11)

Did even Moses and Aaron doubt that the Lord would do what he promised? One biblical tradition says they did, and the Lord said to them:

"Because you did not believe in me, to sanctify me in the eyes of the people of Israel, therefore you shall not bring this assembly into the land which I have given them."
(Numbers 20:12)

This is indeed what happened. The children of Israel left Kadesh for Mount Hor, on the border of Edom. When they arrived, Aaron, the first high priest, died. Moses took care to take his priestly robes and vestments to give to Aaron's son Eleazar, who succeeded him.

But the Israelites' trials continued. The land of Edom refused them passage across its territories, and they had to make a long detour around it. During that journey, the people rebelled once again, and so "then the Lord sent fiery serpents among the people, and they bit the people, so that many people of Israel died."

Once again, Moses had to intercede:

And the Lord said to Moses, "Make a fiery serpent, and set it on a pole; and every one who is bitten, when he sees it, shall live." So Moses made a bronze serpent, and set it on a pole; and if a serpent bit any man, he would look at the bronze serpent and live.

(Numbers 21:8-9)

55 Psalm 95 is a prayer in which the people recorded memories of forty years in the desert. They sang of God's greatness and of God's judgment on unfaithfulness.

Psalm 95 is an invitation to praise God for the blessings not only of creation but especially for that salvation which began when God rescued his people out of bondage in Egypt. This psalm refers back to the Israelites' crossing of the desert. Then, suddenly, it changes its tone, as the author remembers how the people of Israel had been unfaithful to God. The Psalm ends on a sad note: "They shall not enter into my rest."

Psalm 95
O come, let us sing to the Lord;
   let us make a joyful noise to the
      rock of our salvation!
Let us come into his presence with thanksgiving;
   let us make a joyful noise to him
      with songs of praise!
For the Lord is a great God,
   and a great King above all gods.
In his hand are the depths of the earth;
   the heights of the mountains are his also.
The sea is his, for he made it;
   for his hands formed the dry land.

O come, let us worship and bow down,
   let us kneel before the Lord, our Maker!

What does this pitiless judgment mean, coming from a God of mercy? One thing it may mean is that the people to whom God promised the land was not limited to a single generation. Some scholars, as a result, hold that the entire generation of Israelites born in Egypt was indeed unworthy to enter the Promised Land. They had been part of a civilization given over to other gods than the Lord, and they had, in fact, been unfaithful to God in the desert.

Maybe this explains the incredible period of forty years that the Israelites spent in the desert. Imagine: forty years! Actually, forty is a round number used frequently in the Bible; it really means "the amount of time that God wills." In the case of the generation of the Exodus, forty years meant the time required for that generation to renew and purify itself.

For he is our God,
    and we are the people of his pasture,
      and the sheep of his hand.

O that today you would hearken to his voice!
    Harden not your hearts, as at Meribah,
      as on the day at Massah in the wilderness,
when your fathers tested me,
    and put me to the proof, though
      they had seen my work.
For forty years I loathed that generation
    and said, "They are a people who
      err in heart,
    and they do not regard my ways."
Therefore I swore in my anger
    that they should not enter my rest.

56 An old legend tells how Balak, king of Moab, feared Israel. He asked the sorcerer Balaam to curse the Israelites. In the end, Balaam gave to the people of God not a curse but a blessing.

During the time the Israelites were in the desert, Balak, king of Moab, feared that the children of Israel would slowly take over more and more of his territory. So he sent messengers to Pethor on the Euphrates River, to a man named Balaam.

The messengers were important Moabites, and Balaam, to whom they were sent, was a very curious figure in the Bible. He was a kind of sorcerer, a seer who possessed a fearful power to bring about misfortune to his enemies. King Balak of Moab hoped that Balaam would curse the children of Israel and thus reduce their power to nothing. However, it turned out that Balaam — who was not even an Israelite — nevertheless venerated Yahweh with great respect.

Thus it was, then, that Yahweh approached Balaam — the Bible story doesn't say how — and formally forbade him to curse Israel. So Balak's messengers returned to Balak to tell him the bad news. Balak, however, didn't get discouraged. He sent an even more impressive delegation, consisting of princes and other important persons, to try to convince Balaam. But Balaam was no more ready than before to curse Israel, even though the Moabite princes promised him the greatest of honors.

Eventually, Balaam did decide to go with the delegation, though, and, mounted on an ass, he set out, accompanied by two servants. At that point, an angel of the Lord holding a sword stationed himself in Balaam's path. Balaam didn't see the angel; what happened was that his ass refused to go forward. By fits and starts, the ass attempted to move off the path and proceed across the open fields. The seer struck the animal to keep him on the path. The angel moved ahead and stopped at a narrow place on the path where it ran through vineyards with a wall on either side of it. The ass saw the angel in the path and, frightened, pushed into one of the

walls, pressing Balaam's foot against it. Annoyed at such strange behavior, the seer beat the ass with a stick, but succeeded in getting the animal to advance only a very short way. The angel moved ahead to an even narrower place in the path where it was impossible to ride further, and there was no way to turn either to the left or to the right. At this point the ass stopped completely and lay down under Balaam, who beat the animal mercilessly with his stick.

Then the ass—suddenly and marvelously—began to speak: "What have I done to you, that you have struck me these three times?"

Balaam was so beside himself with anger that he showed no surprise at the fact that an ass had spoken. He explained to the ass why he had struck him, "Because you've made a fool of me. I wish I had a sword in my hands, for then I would kill you."

The ass replied, "Am I not the same ass you've ridden on all your life? Did I ever act this way before?"

Balaam replied, "No."

Then Yahweh opened the eyes of Balaam. He saw the angel of the Lord in the path and understood why the ass had balked at going that way.

After all these delays, Balaam finally arrived in Edom with his escort of princes and met Balak. Several times in the course of sacrifices offered by him he received orders directly from Yahweh. These orders said that not only was Balaam not to curse Israel but he was to shower Israel with blessings. He thus did bless Israel with words such as "How fair are your tents, O Jacob, your encampments, O Israel. Like valleys that stretch afar, like gardens beside a river, like aloes the Lord has planted" (Numbers 24:5-6).

King Balak was furious at Balaam, from whom he had obtained nothing, and asked him to depart as soon as possible, scolding him by saying, "Didn't I offer you the greatest honors?"

Balaam admitted this was true, but he said, "Did I not tell your messengers whom you sent to me, 'If Balak should give me his house full of silver and gold, I would not be able to go beyond the word of the Lord, to do either good or bad of my own will: what the Lord speaks, that will I speak" (Numbers 24:12-13).

Then Balaam rose and returned home. Balak, too, went on his way.

57 Moses appointed Joshua
as his successor.
Then, before he died,
Moses saw from Mount Nebo
the land he would never enter.

The amazing, never-to-be-forgotten journey across the desert towards the Promised Land was drawing to a close. Moses was now 120 years old. The Book of Deuteronomy assures us that the old prophet retained both his sight and his vigor. Nevertheless, Moses knew that it was time to be thinking about his successor. It was time to say his goodbyes. Addressing himself to Israel, he declared: "I am no longer capable of fulfilling my duty." And he prayed to God: "Lord God, source of all life, appoint, I pray, a man who can lead the people and can command them in battle, so that your community will not be like sheep without a shepherd." The Lord said to Moses, "Take Joshua son of Nun, a capable man, and place your hands on his head. Have him stand in front of Eleazar the priest and the whole community, and there before them all proclaim him as your successor. Give him some of your own authority, so that the whole community of Israel will obey him" (Numbers 27:16-20 TEV).

The Lord said to Moses, "Go up Mount Abarim and look out over the land that I am giving to the Israelites. After you have seen it, you will die, as your brother Aaron did, because both of you rebelled against my command in the wilderness of Zin. When the whole community complained against me at Meribah, you refused to acknowledge my holy power before them." (Meribah is the spring at Kadesh in the wilderness of Zin.) Then the Lord said to Moses, "This is the land that I promised Abraham, Isaac, and Jacob I would give to their descendants. I have let you see it, but I will not let you go there" (Numbers 27:12-14 TEV; Deuteronomy 34:4 TEV).

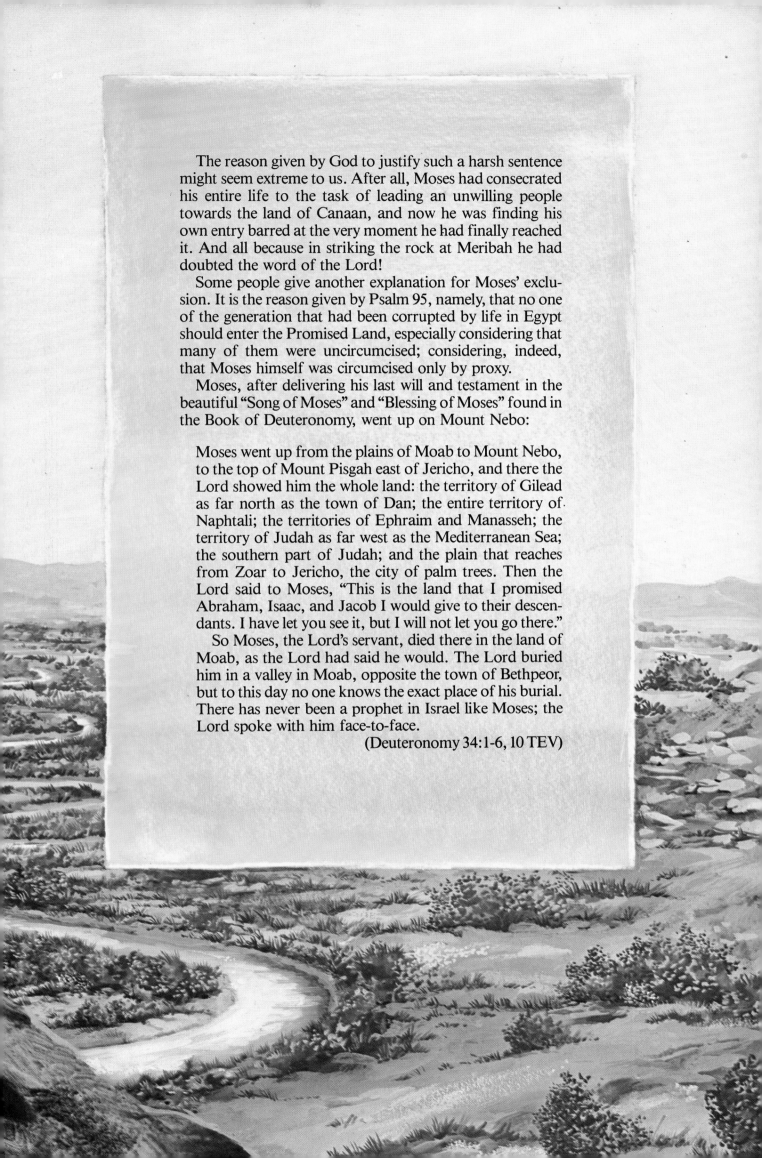

The reason given by God to justify such a harsh sentence might seem extreme to us. After all, Moses had consecrated his entire life to the task of leading an unwilling people towards the land of Canaan, and now he was finding his own entry barred at the very moment he had finally reached it. And all because in striking the rock at Meribah he had doubted the word of the Lord!

Some people give another explanation for Moses' exclusion. It is the reason given by Psalm 95, namely, that no one of the generation that had been corrupted by life in Egypt should enter the Promised Land, especially considering that many of them were uncircumcised; considering, indeed, that Moses himself was circumcised only by proxy.

Moses, after delivering his last will and testament in the beautiful "Song of Moses" and "Blessing of Moses" found in the Book of Deuteronomy, went up on Mount Nebo:

Moses went up from the plains of Moab to Mount Nebo, to the top of Mount Pisgah east of Jericho, and there the Lord showed him the whole land: the territory of Gilead as far north as the town of Dan; the entire territory of Naphtali; the territories of Ephraim and Manasseh; the territory of Judah as far west as the Mediterranean Sea; the southern part of Judah; and the plain that reaches from Zoar to Jericho, the city of palm trees. Then the Lord said to Moses, "This is the land that I promised Abraham, Isaac, and Jacob I would give to their descendants. I have let you see it, but I will not let you go there."

So Moses, the Lord's servant, died there in the land of Moab, as the Lord had said he would. The Lord buried him in a valley in Moab, opposite the town of Bethpeor, but to this day no one knows the exact place of his burial. There has never been a prophet in Israel like Moses; the Lord spoke with him face-to-face.

(Deuteronomy 34:1-6, 10 TEV)

58 The children of Israel were
finally about to enter
the Promised Land.
Psalm 105 is an ancient prayer
that recalls the mighty deeds
accomplished by the Lord
in liberating Israel
from slavery in Egypt
and bringing Israel
across the desert.

Give thanks to the Lord,
    proclaim his greatness;
  tell the nations what he has done.
Sing praise to the Lord;
  tell the wonderful things he has done.
Be glad that we belong to him;
  let all who worship him rejoice.
Go to the Lord for help;
  and worship him continually.
You descendants of Abraham, his servant;
  you descendants of Jacob,
    the man he chose:
remember the miracles that God
    performed
  and the judgments that he gave.

The Lord is our God;
  his commands are for all the world.
He will keep his covenant forever,
  his promises for a thousand generations.
He will keep the agreement
    he made with Abraham
  and his promise to Isaac.
The Lord made a covenant with Jacob,
  one that will last forever.
"I will give you the land of Canaan," he said.
  "It will be your own possession."

God's people were few in number,
  strangers in the land of Canaan.
They wandered from country to country,
  from one kingdom to another.
But God let no one oppress them;
  to protect them, he warned the kings:
"Don't harm my chosen servants;
  do not touch my prophets."

The Lord sent famine to their country
  and took away all their food.
But he sent a man ahead of them,
  Joseph, who had been sold as a slave.
His feet were kept in chains,
  and an iron collar was around his neck,
  until what he had predicted came true.
The word of the Lord proved him right.
Then the king of Egypt had him released;
  the ruler of nations set him free.

He put him in charge of his government
and made him ruler of all the land,
with power over the king's officials
and authority to instruct his advisers.

Then Jacob went to Egypt
and settled in that country.
The Lord gave many children to his people
and made them stronger than their
enemies.
He made the Egyptians hate his people
and treat his servants with deceit.

Then he sent his servant Moses,
and Aaron, whom he had chosen.
They did God's mighty acts
and performed miracles in Egypt.
God sent darkness on the country,
but the Egyptians did not obey his
command.
He turned their rivers into blood
and killed all their fish.
Their country was overrun with frogs;
even the palace was filled with them.
God commanded, and flies and gnats
swarmed throughout the whole country.
He sent hail and lightning on their land
instead of rain;
he destroyed their grapevines and fig trees
and broke down all the trees.
He commanded, and the locusts came,
countless millions of them;

they ate all the plants in the land;
they ate all the crops.
He killed the first-born sons
of all the families of Egypt.

Then he led the Israelites out;
they carried silver and gold,
and all of them were healthy and strong.
The Egyptians were afraid of them
and were glad when they left.
God put a cloud over his people
and a fire at night to give them light.
They asked, and he sent quails;
he gave them food from heaven to
satisfy them.
He opened a rock, and water gushed out,
flowing through the desert like a river.
He remembered his sacred promise
to Abraham his servant.

So he led his chosen people out,
and they sang and shouted for joy.
He gave them the lands of other peoples
and let them take over their fields,
so that his people would obey his laws
and keep all his commands.

Praise the Lord!   (Psalm 105 TEV)

59 Here are some important ideas
in the story
of our early faith ancestors:
  covenant
  desert
  faith
  law
  liberation and redemption
  Passover and Easter

Covenant

God and human beings, hand in hand. That is what the covenant is. It runs like a thread through the entire history of Israel. In this love pact between God and God's people, God is the one who takes the first step. He makes a promise and keeps it. The person who is offered the covenant agrees to live according to its terms.

God, in the covenant with Abraham, promises Abraham numerous descendants and the possession of a Promised Land. God also offers his own friendship and a blessing to be given to all peoples through Abraham. Abraham, for his part, is asked to keep his faith in the one true God and to teach this faith to his descendants.

In the covenant concluded at Mount Sinai between God and the people of Israel, God not only promises to the people their destined land but also protection from all their enemies. Meanwhile, the people of Israel agree to be faithful to God and to observe God's law. But the two participants in the covenant are very different: God is unfailing and perfect, and human beings are weak and imperfect. Human beings are capable of betrayal. (That's what sin really is — a broken word.) The history of Israel tells about a succession of covenants established by God, broken by a sinning people, and renewed through God's constant love.

Desert

Domain ruled by the sun, expanse of blowing sand. And, at the horizon, dunes and fiery mountains. This is the desert, realm of beauty.

But the desert is also a place requiring endurance. Test of hunger and thirst, of eyes that burn. Test of the Exodus. As they went out of Egypt, the followers of Moses experienced hunger, thirst, and fatigue in the Sinai Desert. They experienced temptations to revolt against Moses' leadership and to worship idols. And years later, just before beginning his public life, in the white sands of the Judean desert, Jesus himself experienced temptations of pride and idolatry.

The desert is also the place of encounter with the Lord. For instance, Moses had a conversation with the Eternal One amidst the lightning of Sinai. John the Baptizer prayed in the desert of Judea, getting ready for his mission. And finally, Jesus communed with his Father in the silence of the desert. No silence is quite like the silence of the desert!

Faith

In the dullness and difficulties of everyday life, in the midst of clouds, to believe that the sun can bring light into each one of our days — that is faith.

In this world of violence and war, in the height of the storm, to believe that the dawn of Peace can rise — that is faith.

Faith is trust in people. Trust in God. Just as in the lives of Abraham and Moses, of kings such as David, of prophets and apostles, of Mary, mother of Jesus Christ, of saints such as Francis of Assisi, faith is openness to God, who reveals the beauty of his kingdom of love. Faith is an ever-greater obedience to the Gospel, which calls us to live faithfully in communion with all Christians who are a part of the one body of Christ: the Church.

Law

Laws are necessary. Everyone is supposed to know them and apply them. Often written in grim and forbidding language, they tell what one *must* do as well as what one is *not allowed* to do. The laws of a country are generally made for the common good. They enable people to live with others in society.

In the Bible, however, the law tells what God expects of individuals, particularly of believers. There are three steps in the revelation of the law:

1) On Sinai, the Lord gives to Moses the Ten Commandments. They are the basis for all the numerous other laws which developed over the years among the Israelites.

2) The prophets constantly point out the spirit of the law of God. In the seventh century before Jesus, the Israelite King Josiah brought about a major reform of the law, which is contained in the Book of Deuteronomy. It is here that this important command is found:

Hear, O Israel: The Lord our God is one Lord; and you shall love the Lord your God with all your heart, and with all your soul, and with all your might. (Deuteronomy 6:4-5)

3) Jesus himself repeats this commandment of love, saying that it sums up both the law and the prophets. Just before his death, Jesus declared, "This is my commandment, that you love one another as I have loved you" (John 15:12).

Liberation and Redemption

"From the hand of the oppressor, deliver me, Lord!" This prayer, often repeated in the psalms in slightly different words, sums up well the story of the people of Israel, indeed the story of all humanity.

The oppressor is anyone who does violence, who enslaves. The people of God experienced slavery in Egypt in the time of the pharaohs. Later they had to pay heavy taxes to the countries, such as Assyria, who held them in bondage. They were oppressed during the Babylonian captivity, and for centuries they were dominated by other peoples, such as the Persians, the Greeks, and the Romans.

The oppressor is also anyone who does violence to himself or herself. He or she makes a personal prison, a prison of sin.

In the face of any forms of slavery, God is the liberator. The word *redemption*, which means "buying back," is used often to express the saving action of God. Clearly, the Savior above all others is Jesus.

The Passover and Easter

The passover is the name given to God's "passing over" of the Israelites when he struck down the firstborn of the Egyptians. It is also the name of a celebration observed by the people of Israel. They remember God's saving them in the Exodus and establishing them as a free people. The Passover is celebrated every year during the full moon at the beginning of spring.

Each year, on the Sunday following the full moon of spring, Christians also celebrate a feast — Easter. It is the feast of the Resurrection of Jesus. We celebrate Jesus' passage through death to life, which enables us to pass through death to life. Jesus' passage also allows us to pass from the slavery of sin to the freedom of his love.

Outline by Chapter

THE PATRIARCHS AND MOSES

CHAPTERS

1 The Israelites tell
stories about patriarchs;
Scribes later write them down

2 Middle-East civilizations
flourishing around 1800 B.C.

3 Abram lives near Ur;
Family and tribal structures

4 The city of Ur

5 Abram moves to Haran;
The Lord's call to Abram

6 Abram and Sarai in Canaan
and Egypt;
The promise of land;
Abram and Lot separate

7 Four kings in Canaan;
Abram rescues Lot;
Melchizedek offers a sacrifice

8 How God is revealed to people

9 The covenant between God and Abram,
according to the Yahwist tradition

10 Ishmael is born
to Abram and Hagar

11 The covenant between God and Abram,
according to the priestly tradition

12 Three strangers visit Abraham and Sarah
and predict a son born to them

13 Abraham argues for innocent people
in Sodom

14 Sodom is destroyed

15 Hagar and Ishmael are banished

16 God asks Abraham to sacrifice Isaac

17 Rebekah marries Isaac

18 Jacob and Esau;
Esau sells his birthright

19 Jacob tricks Isaac
into blessing him, not Esau

20 Jacob dreams about a ladder to heaven;
God promises to be with Jacob

21 Jacob works for Laban
to win Rachel

22 Jacob wrestles with God;
Jacob and Esau make peace

23 Jacob makes a pilgrimage

24 Joseph—a just and merciful man

25 Joseph is sold
to a passing caravan

26 Joseph is sold as a slave
and wrongfully sent to prison

27 Joseph interprets Pharaoh's dream

28 The brothers travel to Egypt;
Simeon is kept as hostage

29 Joseph tests his brothers

30 Joseph and his brothers are reunited

31 Jacob and his sons move to Goshen;
Jacob dies

32 The Egyptians make slaves
of the Israelites

33 Egypt—an ancient land
with a highly-developed civilization

34 Pharaoh worsens the condition
of the Israelite slaves

35 Moses is raised by Pharaoh's family;
Moses kills an Egyptian overseer

36 Moses lives in Midian;
God appears in a burning bush

37 God calls Moses to lead
the Chosen People

38 Moses, with Aaron, asks
Pharaoh for time to worship